POP MUSIC

Question & Answer book

Julia Winterson

Peters Edition Limited

Hinrichsen House
10–12 Baches Street
London
N1 6DN

Tel: 020 7553 4000
Fax: 020 7490 4921
email: sales@editionpeters.com
internet: www.editionpeters.com

First published 2005

ISBN 1-84367-014-3

A catalogue record for this book is
available from the British Library

Design and layout by Peter Nickol
Printed in England by Halstan & Co, Amersham, Bucks
Cover design by Joy FitzSimmons after an idea by Jessica Winterson

The publishers would like to thank Andy Collyer, Simon Pitt, Simon Foxall and Robert Faulkner for their assistance during the preparation of this book.

Contents

Introduction

This book has been designed to help teachers and students of pop music at all levels. It caters for the different demands of Rockschool, GCSE and A-Level Music, A-Level Music Technology, BTEC First and National Music Practice or Music Technology Diplomas, as well as undergraduate pop music courses.

A chart on page 46 indicates the suitability of different sections for relevant examinations. However, teachers and students will find that they can often adapt questions and assignments to meet their individual needs.

The first section of the book, 'Coping with exam questions', gives tips and briefings on how to tackle pop music questions and assignments, and provides model answers for analyses, comparisons, and questions on technology and recording techniques.

Analytical listening questions can, with care, be applied to examples of many different periods or styles of music. The generic questions on pages 8–9 cover a range of musical elements, and can be adapted by the teacher or student as appropriate, especially in conjunction with the 'tips and briefings' on the preceding pages.

Most chapters have a selection of Quick Questions, Listening Questions, Essays, and Research Assignments. Answers to the Quick Questions and Listening Questions can be found at the back of the book. It is not within the scope of this book to provide longer answers to the essay questions and research assignments, but the companion volume *Pop Music: the Text Book* provides a useful reference resource. *Pop Music: the Text Book* is available from music shops, bookshops or direct from Peters Edition: www.editionpeters.com

There are questions here on all major musical styles from the origins of pop music onwards. Questions and assignments on music technology are found under three headings: the History of Recording, Electronic Instruments and Digital Technology. The Style and Structure chapter takes examples from a range of periods and styles, concentrating on structural aspects. There is also a page of questions on Acoustic Instruments (mainly guitar and drums), and a page on the Music Business.

Briefings

In this introductory section we consider what to listen for and how to describe it. You will find here guidance as to the types of answers and observations often required. Model answers to style/structure-type questions are shown on pages 10–12, and to technology-type questions on pages 13–14. You should also look at the generic questions on pages 8–9 and try applying these to a wide range of songs; this will help you to sharpen up your analytical and critical listening.

Melody

An **interval** is the distance between two notes. Two notes next to each other (e.g. C and D) are a second apart, two notes with a note in between (e.g. C and E) are a third apart, and so on.

Phrases are sections of music, or sections of a melody, and are often of the same length, e.g. 2-bar phrases, or 4-bar phrases.

Many musical terms are in Italian. The term **legato** is an Italian word for smooth, whereas **staccato** means detached. 'Blue suede shoes' uses a lot of staccato notes whereas another Elvis Presley song, 'Love me tender', is much more legato.

The **range** of a melody refers to the distance between the highest and the lowest notes of the tune. The Beatles songs that were written for Ringo Starr to sing tend to have a narrow range; 'Yellow submarine' has a range of only five notes, with repeated notes and stepwise movement. It is built from short two-bar phrases. In comparison, another Beatles song, 'I saw her standing there', has a range of thirteen notes and includes some wide leaps.

Harmony and key

Most songs are in a major or minor key throughout. Generally speaking minor keys tend to sound sadder than major keys – though there are many exceptions, and many ways in which a major-key song might be made to sound sad.

When a song changes key it is said to have **modulated.** Sometimes a song will start in a major key and end in a minor key (or the other way round). Some chord sequences are very common and easy to recognize e.g. the 12-bar blues. Many songs have repeated chord sequences. In such cases it is worth mentioning that there is a repeated chord sequence even if you cannot pinpoint what the chords are.

Rhythm

The great majority of pop songs have two, three or four beats in a bar – and most have four beats. The most common time signature is **4/4** – this means that there are four crotchet beats in a bar. If you have the sheet music for a song, you will find the **time signature** at the beginning of the first line. If you are listening to a song, listen out for the strong beats which come at the beginning of each bar, and then count how many beats there are in each bar.

When off-beats are accented, the music is said to be **syncopated.** Syncopation is common in pop music, and even more common in jazz.

Reggae music normally accents beats 2 and 4 of each bar, rather than beats 1 and 3, which are traditionally thought of as the strong beats.

When you are describing a rhythm, do not only talk about note lengths. It may be helpful to talk in terms of repeated rhythms, syncopated rhythms, dotted rhythms, accented beats, 'empty' beats (rests), drum breaks and fills, etc.

Tempo

The tempo of a song is simply the speed of the underlying beat. It can be described in words such as fast, slow, moderate – or in Italian terms such as **allegro** (fast), **adagio** (slow) or **moderato** (moderate). It can also be worked out in bpm (beats per minute). You can usually work out the bpm – approximately at least – by looking at the second hand (or digits) on your watch. This will give you 60bpm. A beat that is twice as fast will be 120bpm, and so on.

Form or structure

Many pop songs are in verse-and-chorus form. Some, especially early rock 'n' roll songs, are in 12-bar blues form.

Musical structures can often be described using letternames (A, B, C etc.), where a new lettername identifies a new section of music, usually a different melody and/or chord sequence. In this way, the three-line verse of a 12-bar blues can be described as AAB, because the first two lines are the same and the third is different.

Many songs use an AABA form, perhaps for the verse, or perhaps for the song as a whole. The B section is sometimes described as the **middle eight**. It is a contrasting section (not necessarily eight bars long), and is usually differentiated by being played by different instruments, or by having a different melody or chord sequence. The words may also have a different subject.

Much dance music is a collage of samples and loops. The main sections of dance music can usually be identified as mix in, main section, breakdown and mix out. A **mix in** is an opening section where the DJ mixes the previous track into the new one, while a **mix out** is correspondingly a closing section where the DJ starts to mix in the next track. Both are usually very rhythmic, often using only drums.

A **riff** is a short, repeated melodic pattern, often forming the background to a solo or vocal line, or to a whole song. It is usually 1–4 bars long. The opening of Nirvana's 'Smells like teen spirit' opens with a riff played by a single guitar before the whole band repeats it. A **hook** is a short catchy melodic idea designed to be instantly memorable, as for instance in 'Stuck on you' (Elvis Presley), 'Karma chameleon' (Culture Club), 'Firestarter' (Prodigy), or 'Whole lotta love' (Led Zeppelin).

An **intro** is normally a short instrumental introduction to a song. It can take any form; a striking example is the single chord that opens the Beatles' 'A hard day's night'. Many intros consist of a riff or short chord sequence, leading to the vocal entry.

An outro or **coda** brings a song to a close. Many songs end with the last 2–4 bars repeating and then fading out.

Dynamics

Dynamics are degrees of loud and soft. Sometimes dynamics are contrasted, whole sections being loud or soft: an extreme example is Björk's 'Oh so quiet'. When the music gradually gets louder this is known as a **crescendo**. When it gets softer it is a **diminuendo**. The climax of a song (if there is one) is usually the loudest point, and often occurs about two-thirds or three-quarters way through the song.

Technology

Music technology will typically be found in the use of electronic instruments (e.g. synthesizer, drum machine), samples and loops, effects processing (phasing, flanging, delay, reverb, etc.). Mixing techniques – use of EQ, panning, and relative levels – are important factors. Analogue and digital recording can sometimes be distinguished by the clarity of sound of digital recording.

For model answers to technology questions see pages 13–14.

Instrumentation, timbre and texture

The **instrumentation** simply refers to the instruments and voices used. The **texture** of a piece of music is an overall description of the sound. The description may be in terms of how many layers there are, whether the music is dense or sparse, whether it uses mainly chords or single notes, whether it is continuous or spaced out, and so on. The **timbre** is the instrumental colour: the quality that makes one sound (e.g. a steel-stringed guitar) different from another (e.g. a nylon-stringed guitar). Instruments can produce different sounds or colours through a range of playing techniques and effects. Vocal timbre differs from one singer to another: think of the difference between the gravelly tones of Rod Stewart and the much purer sound of Dido.

Style

The style of the music refers to whether it is punk, funk, soul, rock 'n' roll, or whatever. To describe the main typical musical characteristics of any style, think about instruments, rhythms, playing techniques, forms, chord sequences, and so on. The decade that a song comes from can often be identified by the style and recording techniques used. The mood of a song is usually determined by the words and vocal delivery, and reflected in the music. A sad song may be slow and/or quiet and/or in a minor key.

Generic Listening Questions

The generic questions below are designed to provide useful practice in critical listening. These questions can be applied to the majority of songs, but not every question can be applied to every song. For questions specific to individual songs see the Listening Questions within each of the historical chapters (starting on pages 16, 20, 22, 25, 28, 31), and also in the Style and Structure chapter (pages 41–44).

Melody

What is the interval between the first two notes of the song?
What is the interval between the last two notes?
How long are the phrase lengths?
Is the opening phrase legato or staccato?
What is the range of the melody?

Harmony

Is the song in a major or a minor key?
Describe the chord sequence.

Rhythm

How many beats are there in each bar?
What is the time signature?
Where can you find an example of syncopation?
What is the rhythm of the bass line?

Tempo

What is the approximate tempo of this song?

(a) 30 bpm
(b) 60 bpm
(c) 120 bpm
(d) 240 bpm

Form or structure

Which of the following best describes the form of this song?

(a) 12-bar blues
(b) verse and chorus
(c) theme and variations
(d) collage
(Or: In what form is this song?)

What is the structure of the verse? (AABA etc)
How does the middle eight differ from the verse in this song?
Describe the hook.
Describe the riff.
Describe the introduction (or intro).
Describe the outro (or coda).
Describe the last few bars.
How does the song end?

Dynamics

Describe the dynamics of the song.
Where does the climax come in this song?
Where can you find a crescendo?
Where can you find a diminuendo?
Give an example of dynamic contrast in the song.

Technology

In which decade do you think that this song was recorded? Give two reasons for your answer.
Identify four ways in which music technology is used in this song (or dance track).
Identify two recording effects that have been used on this track.
Briefly describe three of the technological resources that have been used in this track.
Where can you find a use of a sample in this song?
Where can you find a use of a loop in this song?
Identify a place where a particular effect is used e.g. echo, reverb.

Instrumentation, timbre and texture

How would you describe the texture of this music?
What is the vocal range of this song?
How would you describe the singer's voice quality?
Name all the instruments playing.
(Or: Name three of the instruments playing.)
Name one instrument that plays a solo.
Name three instruments which provide the bass and rhythm.
Are any particular or unusual playing techniques used?

Style

What is the name of this style of music?
What are the main musical characteristics of this style?
What decade does this song come from? Give reasons for your answer.
Describe the mood of this music. How do the musical elements combine to create this mood?
How does the music reflect the meaning of the lyrics?

Model Answers

Essays or analyses

Sometimes you will be asked to write an analysis of a particular song in continuous prose. The headings below will help to focus your thoughts and structure your answer.

Style: describe the genre and how it relates to other music either by the same artist or by other artists.

Structure: describe the melodic, rhythmic, harmonic and structural elements.

Instrumentation and texture: describe the instruments, how they are used and their effect on the overall sound.

Performance: describe and evaluate the performance in terms of musicianship (fluency) and communication (what it conveys to the listener).

Technology: describe and evaluate the uses of technology and their effectiveness.

Here is an analysis of 'Wonderwall' (as recorded by Oasis in 1995), following the template above.

Oasis are a Britpop band. Britpop was a nostalgic movement, looking back to the heyday of British pop music in the 1960s, and to bands like the Kinks, the Who and especially the Beatles. Oasis is centred on the brothers Liam and Noel Gallagher, who were highly influenced by the Beatles, the Sex Pistols and the Smiths. The main vocalist, Liam, has likened himself to a cross between John Lennon and Johnny Rotten. Oasis attempted to fuse the aggressive attitude of punk with the melodic songwriting style of Lennon and McCartney.

'Wonderwall' has a moderate tempo of about 90bpm. There are four beats in a bar. The song is in verse and chorus form and is in a minor key. It has three verses, an intro and an outro. The form of the verse is AAB - three phrases, each two bars long. The melodic range is an octave, with the first two phrases of the melody in mainly stepwise movement. The intro opens with the four-chord sequence that is used for each line of the verse. A new chord sequence is introduced in the chorus. There is a dramatic pause after the first chorus - in some ways this could be described as the climax of the song. The melodies of both the verse and the chorus use syncopated rhythms. The outro ends with a held chord followed by a guitar arpeggio apparently unrelated to the song - almost as though an accident has been left in for effect.

This song is scored for lead vocal and backing vocals, acoustic, electric and bass guitar, strings and piano. Essentially this is the same line-up as was used by many groups in the 1960s. Oasis have a very distinctive guitar-driven sound, a dense texture with chiming guitars. The opening is striking, using strummed acoustic guitar. The bass and drums play similar rhythmic patterns throughout. The texture is built up in layers: the strings and drums enter in verse 2, to great effect, and the backing vocals are not used until the final chorus. Other interesting features are the long-note cello countermelody and the strategically-placed drum entry which appears after the word 'backbeat'. A piano plays a prominent part in the outro with a repeated five-note figure.

'Wonderwall' is a simple love song. Liam Gallagher has a soulful voice with an excellent sense of phrasing, particularly evident in the sustained long notes in the chorus. Oasis portray a hard, thuggish image, and this aggression is reflected to some extent in the hard edge of his slightly sneering vocal style.

The same dynamic level prevails through most of the song. The vocal line is well forward in the mix, along with the sustained cello notes. Otherwise the mix is down the middle of the stereo field - possibly to reflect the mono mixes of the 1960s. The sound fades as it approaches the dramatic pause after the first chorus, effectively drawing more attention to it. The strange effect of the final quiet guitar arpeggio is heightened by added effects.

Analytical comparisons

Sometimes you will be asked to make a comparison between two songs or two different versions of the same song. The table below provides a format to help focus your thoughts.

	Version 1	**Version 2**
Instrumentation		
Vocals / Backing vocals		
Texture		
Dynamics		
Style		
Form		

A model answer along these lines is provided on the following page, taking as an example the Bob Dylan song 'All along the watchtower' and comparing Dylan's original recording with the version by Jimi Hendrix.

	Version 1 Bob Dylan as recorded on *John Wesley Harding* (1968)	**Version 2** Jimi Hendrix as recorded on *Electric Ladyland* (1968)
Instrumentation	Acoustic guitar, bass guitar, harmonica and drums	Lead guitar, acoustic rhythm guitar, bass guitar, drums and tambourine.
Vocals / Backing vocals	Folk-like solo singing by Bob Dylan	Jimi Hendrix sings in an urgent, portentous style. The mood is completely different - edgy and exciting.
Texture	Apart from some short harmonica solos in between the verses, the texture remains the same throughout most of the song. The drums play the same simple, regular pattern and the bass guitar repeats the same 2-bar phrase.	The texture is generally dense but the instrumental colours are forever changing with instruments dropping in and out, different guitar sounds and effects, drum fills.
Dynamics	The same moderately quiet dynamic prevails throughout, reflecting the contemplative mood of this version.	There is much use of crescendos and diminuendos, all adding to the intense excitement of this version. Each verse ends with a crescendo drum fill.
Style	This is in a gentle folk-song style with strummed guitar and a simple repeated melody. The lyrics are the most important feature of this version. There are four beats in a bar, and the tempo is quite fast.	The style could be described as psychedelic, with lots of use of virtuosic guitar effects and stereo recording effects, e.g. drum fills panning across from the LH speaker to the RH speaker and guitars duetting between the two speakers. The tempo is slower than Dylan's, but there is a fierce energy throughout the song.
Form	There are three verses each with four lines. Each line has the same melody (AAAA) and is broken up into two 2-bar phrases. The rhyming pattern is AABB. The song opens with a strummed guitar before the drums enter and then the vocals.	The form of the song has been left unaltered, so again there are three 4-line verses formed of 2-bar phrases. The song opens with an 8-bar intro. The lead guitar enters in bar 5 with a decorated version of Dylan's original vocal melody. There is a guitar flourish at the end of each 2-bar phrase of the verse. An extended 32-bar instrumental between verses 2 and 3 uses sounds such as glissandi, wah-wah pedal and stereo effects. A 16-bar instrumental after verse 3 opens with a crescendo on the drums; the second half is an exciting guitar solo, largely on one note.

Technology questions

Example: Listen to 'Love at first sight' (from *Fever*) by Kylie Minogue. How has music technology been used to enhance and realise this song?

Model answer

This song uses technology in a creative way both in terms of the creation of sounds and in the way they have been recorded and mixed. The song, using essentially only three chords, lends itself to a sample-based production, but straightforward repetition has been avoided by clever use of FX and sensitive mixing.

Some rather retro sounds have been employed: the synth line (sounding quite analogue, although undoubtedly produced by a soft synth), the phased guitar and the electronic toms in the introduction, for example. These have been sampled and layered to create a distinct dance-pop feel.

The introduction begins with just the first chord and the drum loop repeated with the higher frequencies gradually filtered in, creating a sense of expectancy. The drum track has a much reduced bass frequency in the middle eight ('and everything went from wrong to right'), lightening the texture in preparation for the chorus, where the rhythm track returns to its original settings.

At the end of the chorus, the entire track is gradually filtered to remove high and middle frequencies, leaving just a vague rhythmic throb such as one might hear from outside a club. The lead vocal floats clearly over the top of this mix for two lines, after which the filtering restores the higher frequencies for the second half of the verse.

In the final middle eight, filtering is used again (rather more rapidly this time) to remove higher frequencies. We hear a heavily phased cymbal, and the backing is reduced to an acoustic guitar sample and a pad. This is followed by a return to the original EQ settings.

Throughout the song, delay is used on the vocals. This is most noticeable on the word 'love' in the chorus, at the beginning of the second verse, and in the final middle eight. Vocals have also been overdubbed by Kylie to produce the three-part harmonies in the chorus and the ad lib vocals in the outro.

Overall, technology has been used in two ways: the choice and layering of samples gives a retro-dance feel, and the filtering and use of delay softens the track and lightens the texture to reflect the romantic lyrical content.

You may be asked to compare different tracks in terms of recording techniques and use of music technology. The table below provides an example of how this type of question might be answered.

Andrews Sisters, 'Bei mir bist du schön' from *Songbirds, Volume 1* (1937)	**Yes, 'Roundabout'** from *Fragile* (1972)	**Madonna, 'Music'** from *Music* (2000)
In this era, recording was somewhat basic, with the recording engineer being largely involved with achieving balance by careful placement of the musicians in relation to the microphone. This often resulted in poor balance, with some instruments sounding distant or poorly focused as in this recording. Stereo technology had not yet been invented, so recordings are in mono (you will hear everything set dead centre on headphones). There is also a tendency to a limited frequency range, again owing to the technology available, which excludes the extreme upper and lower frequency ranges. Distortion is also a recurrent problem with recordings of this period, as you can hear particularly on the vocals in this track.	The recording and mixing techniques used on this track, and indeed its general sonic quality, place it firmly in the 1970s. The use of reverse reverb on the piano (achieved by turning the analogue tape over, recording reverb onto the now reversed piano, and then turning the tape back over, thus hearing the reverb 'backwards') and the sometimes extreme stereo separation, particularly on the analogue synth sounds (the use of which also places the track in this era) are good indicators. The overall sound is warm and shows evidence of analogue recording, but feels slightly muffled in terms of EQ compared with modern digital recordings. There was a tendency not to boost high EQ too much for fear of enhancing tape hiss levels. There is also a small amount of unwanted distortion in the louder sections, which was still not uncommon in this period. There is extensive use of overdubbing in terms of the keyboards (the monophonic synthesizer in particular), percussion and vocals.	This track demonstrates many of the tricks of 21st-century recording and mixing. From the clarity of the recording and the application of editing and FX, it is clearly digital. Notable features include: • The pitch shift on the opening spoken vocal • The vocoder effect on the vocals. The vocoder - a device used to 'blend' a voice and another sound source, usually a synth - was used widely in the 1980s but was re-popularized in the late 90s with Cher's release of 'Believe'. • The use of repetitive sampling, particularly the new vogue for analogue synth sounds (probably created with soft-synths in this case) • Looped samples (Madonna singing the word 'music' for example) along with filtering using protocols or similar software, and the editing of samples into smaller units. The vocal is mixed without reverb (reverb was sometimes used in the past to cover up blemishes on tracks and to hide tape hiss - digital recoding doesn't require this kind of 'cover-up'), and there is a relatively high top-end EQ on the vocal, unlike music of previous eras.

Context

Essays

1 Describe some of the ways in which 'pop' and 'rock' are perceived as different types of music. Do you think it is a valid distinction?

2 In what ways can the term 'popular music' be problematic?

3 'If ever there was a band who thought that their music could change the world, it was U2'. Discuss.

4 List six differences between classical music and popular music?

5 Give a snapshot of teen culture in the 1950s. How would life as a teenager in the 1950s have differed from life as a teenager in the early 21st century?

6 It could be said that the albums *Sergeant Pepper's Lonely Hearts Club Band* and *Never Mind the Bollocks* both sum up the mood of a generation. Do you agree with this? What do the albums tell us about 1960s and 1970s culture?

7 In April 1978 Rock Against Racism held a huge rally in which 100,000 people marched from Trafalgar Square through London's East End – the heart of National Front territory – to a concert in Hackney. On the bill were many celebrated reggae and punk bands of the time. Discuss what this tells us about 1970s politics and music.

Research Assignments

1 Outline some of the ways in which attitudes to popular music have changed in the last fifty years.

2 What part has radio played in the evolution of pop music? Your answer should include reference to some or all of the following: early developments in the history of recording; the Grand Ole Opry; Moondog's Rock and Roll Party; Radio 1; censorship; the charts.

3 Take the lyrics of 'Rock around the clock' and compare these with the lyrics of either a punk song or a gangsta rap song. What conclusions can be drawn about the contextual influences of the two different periods?

4 Twentieth-century technology has meant that the distance between cultures has been closed up, giving wider access to new experiences and possibilities. How has this affected the production, dissemination and content of pop music?

5 Which two albums would you choose to sum up the mood of the 1980s and 1990s? Give three reasons why you have chosen each album.

Origins

Quick Questions

Background information in *Pop Music: the Text Book* pages 9–20

1 List some rhythmic features of African music. Name any aspect of West African music that has been carried over into pop music, giving an example.

2 What is a worksong? Why did worksongs become an important part of African-American culture?

3 What sort of musical entertainment would you have found in nineteenth-century rural America?

4 (a) What is call and response?
(b) Name three styles of music in which call and response can be found.
(c) Give an example of call and response from any song you know.

5 What do you understand by the following?
(a) talking drums
(b) oral tradition

Essays

1 Why was the blues so important in the development of pop music?

2 Describe the worksong and its significance in the development of the blues.

3 In what ways did Louis Armstrong lay the foundations for jazz in 'West End blues'?

4 Discuss the importance of Tin Pan Alley in the development of pop music.

5 Give a profile of a blues artist of your choice.

Listening Questions

1 Listen to any piano ragtime piece by Scott Joplin, for example 'Maple Leaf rag' or 'The entertainer'.
(a) What is the tempo of the piece?
(b) How many beats are there in a bar?
(c) Describe the rhythm used in the left hand.
(d) Describe the rhythm used in the right hand.
(e) How many different themes can you hear?

2 Listen to 'West End blues' played by Louis Armstrong and his Hot Five.
   (a) Describe the structure.
   (b) Which three instruments play in the frontline?
   (c) Which three instruments play in the rhythm section?

3 Listen to any blues song recorded before 1950.
   (a) What key is the song in?
   (b) Which three chords are used throughout most of the song?
   (c) Write out the words of the first verse of the song and mark with a cross where the chord changes.
   (d) Give three features of the song that are typical of the blues.

4 Listen to 'Black and tan fantasy' by Duke Ellington. Explain what you understand by:
   (a) swung rhythm
   (b) syncopation
   (c) substitution chords

   Describe three musical elements you can hear which are now commonly used in pop music.

   This is an early recording. Describe three of the shortcomings in recording techniques in the 1920s and describe how they would be overcome today.

   How is variety added to the 12-bar blues structure this song is based on?

5 Listen to 'Summertime' by George Gershwin. Explain what you understand by:
   (a) chromatic scale
   (b) chromatic harmony
   Give an example of each as found in 'Summertime'.

   Which of the following is the musical form of the verse?
   (a) AABB
   (b) ABAB
   (c) ABAC

6 'Summertime' is a jazz standard and has been recorded by over 2500 different artists including Ella Fitzgerald and Louis Armstrong, Sam Cooke, Sara Vaughan, Robert Palmer, Fun Boy Three and Willie Nelson. Why do you think so many artists have been attracted to this song?

   Compare any two versions using the following format:

	Version 1	**Version 2**
Name of artist		
Instrumentation		
Vocals / Backing vocals		
Texture		
Dynamics		
Style		
Form		

7 Many Tin Pan Alley songs use the 32-bar song form.
   (a) Describe the structure of this form.
   (b) Analyse the 32-bar structure of Gershwin's 'I got rhythm' or any other appropriate song of this era.

8 Listen to 'Four' by Miles Davis. This is an example of bebop (or modern jazz). What are the main stylistic features of bebop?

Describe three of the effects that Miles Davis uses in the trumpet solo.

9 Listen to any gospel choir recording.
   (a) What are the main characteristics of the style?
   (b) Pick any gospel-influenced song produced in the last twenty years and describe the elements that it has taken from gospel music.

10 Listen to 'I'm leavin' you' by Howlin' Wolf. Explain what you understand by:
   (a) stop time (b) blue notes (c) lick (d) triplet
Give an example of each as found in 'I'm leavin' you'.

Write out a minor pentatonic scale in G.

Research Assignments

1 Outline some of the differences between the music taken to America by the European settlers and the music taken there by the African slaves.

2 Which musical characteristics of ragtime might be described as European in origin and which might be described as African in origin?

3 Describe the role played by different types of religious song in the origins of pop music.

4 Outline the main differences between Delta blues and urban blues. Give examples of each.

5 Select two of the following blues artists and write a brief biography. This should describe how they contributed to the development of the blues. Refer to specific recordings in your answer.
   (a) Robert Johnson
   (b) Leadbelly
   (c) W C Handy
   (d) John Lee Hooker
   (e) B B King
   (f) Charley Patton

6 What were vaudeville and music hall? What features do they have in common with pop music?

7 What were the conditions in New Orleans which led to it becoming the first place where jazz became prominent?

8 What part did radio play in the evolution of pop music up to and including the 1950s?

1950s

Quick Questions

Background information in *Pop Music: the Text Book* pages 21–30.

1 What kind of music would you have found in the UK charts in the early 1950s, pre-rock 'n' roll?

2 What are some of the common themes of rock 'n' roll lyrics?

3 Name:
 (a) Two major record labels of the 1950s.
 (b) Two independent record labels of the 1950s.

4 What is skiffle music? Which instruments gave it its characteristic sound?

5 Which of the following is the Bo Diddley beat?

a) 

b) 

c) 

Essays

1 What is Tin Pan Alley? Compare and contrast 1950s Tin Pan Alley music with rock 'n' roll.

2 Five of the most successful US chart albums in 1957 were *Merry Christmas* by Bing Crosby, *Close to You* by Frank Sinatra, *Loving You* by Elvis Presley, *Love is the Thing* by Nat King Cole and the soundtrack to *Around the World in 80 Days.* What does this tell us about popular music in the 1950s?

3 The two main influences on rock 'n' roll were blues and country music. What were the characteristics of each and how did they come together to form rock 'n' roll?

4 How would you account for Elvis Presley's meteoric rise to stardom in the mid 1950s?

5 Read the statement below. How true is it to say that 'Rock around the clock' started pop?

> ...in April 1954 an ageing Country 'n' Western singer called Bill Haley made a record called Rock Around the Clock. By 1955 it was a hit in America and then it was a hit in Britain and then it was a hit all over the world. And it just kept on selling, it wouldn't quit...By the time it was finished, it had sold fifteen million copies. It had also started pop.
>
> Nik Cohn, *Pop*, 1969

Listening Questions

See also questions 1 and 2 on page 41.

1 Listen to 'Rave on' by Buddy Holly.
  (a) Give two features of this song that tell you it is a rock 'n' roll song.
  (b) Describe the tempo.
  (c) Is the song in a major or a minor key?
  (d) This song uses a lot of syncopation. What is syncopation?
  (e) Describe how the song ends.

2 Listen to 'Blue suede shoes' by Carl Perkins.
  (a) This has one of the most memorable intros in pop music. What makes it so memorable?
  (b) Where can you hear the blues influence in this song?
  (c) How would you describe the bass line?
  (d) Describe how the song ends.

3 Listen to 'Maybelline' by Chuck Berry. This contains many of the trademarks of Chuck Berry's style – describe them.

4 Listen to 'Move it' by Cliff Richard. What aspects of US rock 'n' roll did Cliff Richard imitate in this 1958 hit?

5 There are many cover versions of 'Blue suede shoes' by artists including Elvis Presley, the Beatles, Jimi Hendrix, Black Sabbath, Motorhead, Buddy Holly, Bill Haley, Pat Boone and Johnny Hallyday. Compare any two versions using the format below.

	Version 1	**Version 2**
Name of artist		
Instrumentation		
Vocals / Backing vocals		
Texture		
Dynamics		
Style		
Form		
Other comments		

Research Assignment

1 A national newspaper is giving away a free CD called *The Greatest Rock 'n' Roll Songs Ever.* You have been asked to choose six tracks by six different artists from the 1950s. List your six tracks and then write a sleeve note that should include:
  (a) a brief history of the origins of rock 'n' roll
  (b) a couple of sentences about each track
  (c) a couple of sentences about each artist

1960s

Quick Questions

Background information in *Pop Music: the Text Book* pages 31–46.

1 What style of 1960s music would you associate with each of the following places?
   (a) Brill Building
   (b) Greenwich Village
   (c) Jamaica

2 Name three American artists who influenced the British R&B movement.

3 Who was Prince Buster?

4 Match up the songs below with their songwriting teams.

A	Gerry Goffin and Carole King	1	Can't buy me love
B	Lennon and McCartney	2	Up on the roof
C	Burt Bacharach and Hal David	3	Saturday night at the movies
D	Barry Mann and Cynthia Weil	4	Anyone who had a heart

5 What was Phil Spector's 'wall of sound'?

Essays

1 How would you differentiate between pop and rock music in the 1960s?

2 Outline the career of Bob Dylan, describing his early influences, albums, lyrics, and different styles/periods.

3 Describe Bob Dylan's musical style and assess his contribution to pop music in relation to the following assessments:

> He was strange. Technically, he was nothing at all, he played bad guitar and blew bad mouth-harp, he hardly ever sang in tune and his voice was ugly, it came through his nose and whined.
>
> Nik Cohn, *Pop*, 1969

> There's no singer-songwriter in the last thirty-five years who doesn't owe something of their craft to Bob Dylan.
>
> *The Cambridge Companion to Pop and Rock*, ed. Simon Frith 2001

4 Why was *Sergeant Pepper's Lonely Hearts Club Band* so significant in the story of pop?

5 For a time during the 1960s there was an interest in all things Eastern, particularly Indian. How do you account for this? How did it influence the music of the Beatles?

6 Describe the early development and main features of heavy metal. Which artists do you consider crucial to that early development, and why?

Listening Questions

See also questions 3, 4 and 6 on pages 41–42.

1 Listen to 'Stand by me' by Ben E King. Name two features of this soul standard that are typical of soul music.

Which of the following is the form of the song?
(a) verse and chorus
(b) 12-bar blues
(c) collage

How many beats are there in a bar?
(a) two
(b) three
(c) four

Name the instruments used in the intro.

How are dynamics and instrumentation used to build up the excitement?

Which of the following statements best describes the song's harmonic scheme?
(a) It uses a repeated chord sequence.
(b) It is a 12-bar blues.
(c) It is all in a minor key.

2 Listen to 'Can't buy me love' by the Beatles.

Describe the chord sequence of the verse.

Which of the following statements is true?
(a) The verse is in the minor and the chorus is in the major.
(b) The verse is in the major and the chorus is in the minor.
(c) The verse and chorus are both in the minor.

Which of the following shows the pitches of the opening line of the chorus, on the words 'Can't buy me love'?

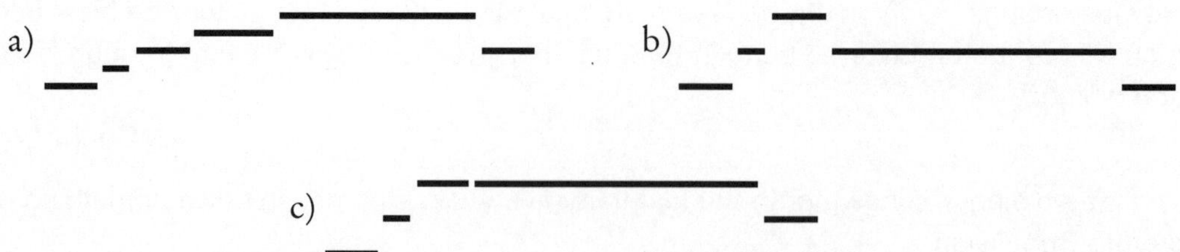

Where does the guitar solo appear?

Identify one line of the song which uses stop time.

3 Listen to 'Help!' by the Beatles.

How is the word 'Help' emphasized?

Describe the backing vocals.

Which of these is the form of the song?

(a) Intro – Verse – Chorus – Verse – Chorus – Verse – Chorus – Coda
(b) Intro – Verse – Chorus – Verse – Chorus – Middle Eight – Chorus – Coda
(c) Verse – Chorus – Verse – Chorus – Verse – Chorus – Coda

4 Listen to 'A day in the life' by the Beatles. In what ways could this song be described as psychedelic?

Give two places where the music clearly reflects the lyrics.

Describe some of the ways in which the middle section of the song (written by Paul McCartney) contrasts with the verses (written by John Lennon).

Describe how the following are used in 'A day in the life':

(a) orchestra
(b) piano
(c) drums

5 Listen to *Highway 61 Revisited* by Bob Dylan. Why was this 1965 LP so significant in the story of pop? Your answer should include reference to at least three songs.

6 Listen to *Pet Sounds* by the Beach Boys.

(a) Brian Wilson wrote that he 'made each track a sound experience of its own'. How did he do this? Take two tracks from the album and refer to production, instrumentation, vocal sound and arrangement in your answer.
(b) Paul McCartney is said to have described 'God only knows' as 'the best song that had ever been written'. What aspects of the song do you think might have appealed to him?

Research Assignments

1 What was the contribution of either Phil Spector or George Martin to pop music in the 1960s? Your answer should include reference to recording techniques and artists, and should look at least one album in some detail.

2 Describe British R&B. What were its roots and influences? Who were some of the bands? What were some of the songs covered?

3 The Beatles were one of the most successful bands ever. Outline some of the elements that account for their success and analyse at least two of their songs in detail.

4 To what extent does the 1969 Woodstock Festival represent a snapshot of late-1960s pop music and culture?

1970s

Quick Questions

Background information in *Pop Music: the Text Book* pages 47–68.

1 With which style of music are each of these three record labels most commonly associated?
Two Tone
Trojan Records
Alternative Tentacles

2 Explain what you understand by the following and give an example of each.
concept album
prog rock
guitar hero

3 Explain what you understand by the following.
dub recording
sound system
toasting
With which style are they all associated?

4 With which style of music are each of the following films associated?
Saturday Night Fever
The Harder They Come
The Great Rock 'n' Roll Swindle
Spinal Tap

5 What is 'Philly soul'?

6 What defines *Dark Side of the Moon* as a 'concept album'?

Essays

1 Describe the typical punk instrumentation and sound. Choose one 1970s punk track to illustrate your answer.

2 The 1970s rock critic Lester Bangs once wrote:

> The essential misapprehension about popular music is that it is anything other than a totally capitalist enterprise. In fact, it has absolutely nothing to do with anything except making money and getting rich. Some popular musicians start out with revolutionary rhetoric, but all they want is cars and girls and champagne.

Discuss this statement with reference to (a) punk and (b) prog rock.

3 Describe the origins of reggae. Make at least five points.

4 Abba had eighteen consecutive Top Ten hits following their success with 'Waterloo' in the 1974 Eurovision Song Contest, and their albums are still selling well. What are the elements of their musical appeal?

Listening Questions

See also questions 5 and 8–11 on pages 42–43.

1 Listen to 'Teenage kicks' by the Undertones.
This song could be described as New Wave. How does New Wave music differ from punk?
Describe the intro to the song.
How many beats are there in a bar?
What is the tempo?
Which of the following shapes best represents the first phrase of the vocal line?

a) --- ▬▬-▬- ▬▬

b) --- ▬▬- ▬- ▬▬

c) --- ▬▬-▬- ▬▬

2 There are many cover versions of 'Teenage kicks', including ones by Busted, Skunk Anansie and the Saw Doctors. Compare any two versions using the format below.

	Version 1	**Version 2**
Name of artist		
Instrumentation		
Vocals / Backing vocals		
Texture		
Dynamics		
Style		
Form		
Other comments		

3 Listen to 'The winner takes it all' by Abba.
Name two elements that have contributed to the success of Abba.
Which instruments can you hear in the opening?
Comment on the rhyming scheme of the lyrics.
At the beginning of which verse do the drums enter?
Name two keyboard sounds/instruments that you can hear.
Describe the melody.
What is it that is so catchy about this song?
Which of these intervals is prominent throughout the song?
(a) fifth
(b) second
(c) fourth
What is the form of the song?
How does the song end?

4 Listen to 'Tupelo honey' by Van Morrison

The whole song is based on a repeated four-chord pattern. How is variety achieved?

Van Morrison's musical style is a fusion of different influences. What musical elements of each of the following styles can you hear?
- (a) soul
- (b) jazz
- (c) Celtic rock

Describe the texture of 'Tupelo honey'.

5 Listen to two albums by David Bowie. Choose one from List A and one from List B. Compare them. How has the musical style of David Bowie changed?

List A
The Rise and Fall of Ziggy Stardust and the Spiders from Mars
Aladdin Sane

List B
Heroes
Young Americans
Diamond Dogs

6 Listen to 'Reynardine' or any other song by Fairport Convention. How would you define folk rock? Refer to the chosen song in your answer.

7 Listen to *What's Going On* by Marvin Gaye
- (a) How does the sound of this album differ from previous Motown records?
- (b) Comment on the vocal sound and use of overdubbing on 'Save the children' or any other song on this album.

Research Assignments

1 You have been asked to compile a CD called *The Golden Age of Disco* to be given away free with a daily newspaper. Choose and list six representative disco tracks from the 1970s. Write a sleeve note that includes:
- (d) a definition of disco
- (e) a brief history of the origins of disco
- (f) a couple of sentences about each track

2 You have been asked to compile a CD called *Let's Party* to be given away free with a daily newspaper. Choose and list six representative glam rock tracks from the 1970s. Write a sleeve note that includes:
- (a) something about when and why glam rock came about
- (b) a description of the glam style and image
- (c) a couple of sentences about each track

3 Trace David Bowie's career, analysing his image and his music. Do you believe that David Bowie's image was as important as his music?

1980s

Quick Questions

Background information in *Pop Music: the Text Book* pages 69–86.

1 Explain what you understand by:
Breaks
Breakdancing

2 Explain what you understand by:
tapping
divebombing

3 What is the 'Balearic beat'? Where would you go to hear it?

4 Complete the following table to show the style of music these record labels are most associated with.

Record label	Style of music
Rough Trade	
Sugarhill Records	
Def Jam	

5 What does four-on-the-floor mean? With what style of music is it most associated?

6 Which city is the birthplace of 'house', and how did the term originate? Which elements of house music can be traced back to disco?

7 Which city is the birthplace of 'garage', and how did the term originate?

8 Name some of the non-musical influences on Goth music.

9 How does the thrash metal of Metallica differ from earlier heavy metal?

10 Name some of the musical and non-musical elements that are part of hip-hop culture.

Essays

1 Assess the importance of MTV and video in 1980s pop music.

2 Outline some of the main differences between house music in the UK and the US.

3 Assess Kraftwerk's contribution to 1980s music.

4 Outline some of the main characteristics of the New Romantic movement.

5 To what extent do you agree with the following statement?

> Rap is the popular form which can best claim some affinity with the blues.
>
> *The Cambridge Companion to Pop and Rock*, ed. Simon Frith, 2001

Outline some of the differences and similarities between rap and blues.

Listening Questions

See also question 13 on page 44.

1 Compare 'Love in a void' with either 'Playground twist' or 'Happy house'. How has the musical style of Siouxsie and the Banshees changed?

2 Listen to 'Love can't turn around' by Jesse Saunders. What elements are typical of house music?

3 Many house and techno tracks are reworkings of earlier songs. Take any 1980s house or techno track which reworks an earlier song and compare the two versions using the format below.

	Version 1	**Version 2**
Name of artist		
Instrumentation		
Vocals / Backing vocals		
Texture		
Use of samples		
Form / Structure		
Style		

4 Listen to 'You think you're a man' by Divine or any other HiNRG track. What are the musical characteristics of HiNRG? Where did it originate?

5 Listen to 'How soon is now' or any other song by the Smiths.
   (a) What are the main features of the Smiths' style? You should refer to songwriting and performance characteristics in your answer.
   (b) How are the Smiths typical of 1980s indie style?

6 Listen to 'Summer of 69' by Bryan Adams. Which three of the following statements are true?
   (a) The song is in the same major key throughout.
   (b) The song changes key in the middle eight.
   (c) The song has four beats in a bar.
   (d) The song opens with the chorus.
   (e) The voice part has a wide range.
   (f) The intro uses repeated quavers.
   (g) The first note the voice sings is the tonic.
   (h) Only two chords are used throughout.

7 Listen to 'Cars' or any other song by Gary Numan. What are the hallmarks of Gary Numan's style?

8 Listen to any song by Joy Division. Describe the elements which contribute to Joy Division's dark, sombre sound and image.

9 Listen to 'I should be so lucky' or any other 1980s hit by Stock, Aitken and Waterman. What are the musical characteristics of the song? Assess the contribution of Stock, Aitken and Waterman to 1980s pop.

Research Assignments

1 How do you account for the rise in club culture that took place in the 1980s? Your answer should include reference to the following three clubs, assessing their significance and outlining the style of music with which they are most associated.
   Billy's
   Pasha
   Warehouse

2 You have been asked to compile a CD to be played at a 1980s retro night.
   (a) Choose six tracks and list them, explaining why you have chosen each one as being representative of the 1980s.
   (b) Describe the outfit that you are going to wear.

3 Three broad categories run through the pop music of the 1980s:
   1 post-punk guitar music
   2 technology-influenced styles including dance and rap
   3 pop styles

State which category each of the four bands below belongs to. Write a paragraph about each band, outlining the features of their style and including a description of an album or song.
   Van Halen   Kraftwerk   Public Enemy   Wham!

4 What are the following?
   (a) a synthesizer
   (b) a drum machine
   (c) a sample

Which styles of 1980s music are they most associated with?
Take any track you know which uses all three of these elements, and describe how they are used.

1990s

Quick Questions

Background information in *Pop Music: the Text Book* pages 87–106.

1 Name two styles of music that have been combined to create bhangra.

2 What are the musical features of ambient or chill-out music? What do these two names mean?

3 What is a rap battle?

4 What is a TB303? Name one song that uses a TB303.

5 What do you understand by the following terms?
   (a) mix in
   (b) mix out
   (c) breakdown
   With what style of music are these terms associated?

Essays

1 Name some of the musical features of the work of the Stone Roses that can be traced back to earlier decades. In what ways did the Stone Roses influence later bands?

2 What are the similarities and differences between Blur and Oasis?

3 What are the defining characteristics, both musical and non-musical, of grunge? The most successful grunge album is Nirvana's *Nevermind*. To what do you attribute its success?

4 Evaluate the role of the DJ within club culture. Look at one sub-genre of dance music in detail, and discuss the technical, cultural and musical elements of the work of the DJ.

5 What is bhangra music? Take any bhangra track that you know and describe two musical features that come from Asia and two musical features that come from the West.

6 How is Eminem's life reflected in his music? Refer to at least two of his albums in your answer. To what do you attribute Eminem's success?

7 The musical career of James Brown has, so far, spanned five decades. Trace James Brown's career since the 1950s and discuss to what extent it reflects the history of pop.

8 The music of Public Enemy could be described as both mass entertainment and minority protest. Choose a Public Enemy track and explain how it illustrates this statement.

Listening Questions

See also questions 12, 14 17 and 18 on pages 43–44.

1 'Killing in the name' by Rage Against the Machine is a fusion of metal and rap.
(a) Describe two features of the track that are derived from metal.
(b) Describe two features of the track that are derived from rap.

2 Listen to 'Stan' by Eminem and Dido.
Describe the main ingredients of the song.
Describe the bass line.
In what ways are the lyrics typical of rap?
This track uses a lot of repetition. Where does the main interest lie?
How are sound effects used in the song?
Name one DJ-ing technique that is used.

3 Listen to 'Let me entertain you' by Robbie Williams.
How would you describe the style of this song?
How many beats are there in a bar?
What makes this song sound so energetic?
How is the excitement built up through the intro?
The words (of the chorus) 'Let me entertain you' are built around one interval. What is the interval?
The line 'Let me entertain you' could be described as a hook. What is a hook?
How does the verse differ rhythmically from the chorus?
How does the use of dynamics add to the song?
How many chords are used in this song?
(a) two
(b) three
(c) four
Name two instruments that you can hear apart from guitar and drums.

4 Listen to 'Angels' by Robbie Williams.
What is the interval between the first two notes of the song?
At which words does the vocal register change?
What is the tempo of the song?
How does the song build up to a climax?

5 Listen to 'Can't get you out of my head' sung by Kylie Minogue
Describe two elements that make this song so catchy.
How are the words reflected in the accompaniment?

6 Listen to 'Don't look back in anger' by Oasis
Explain what you understand by the term Britpop.
Describe three ways in which Oasis may have been influenced by the Beatles in this track.
How does the texture contribute to the unique sound of Oasis?
Where is the climax of the song? How is this climax achieved?
How do the tempo, dynamics and texture change in the last few bars?

7 What features of Britpop are evident in the Pulp song 'Common people'?

8 How are Brian Eno's albums *Discreet Music* and *Music for Airports* typical of ambient music?

9 Compare Roberta Flack's version of 'Killing me softly with his song' with the Fugees' version, using the format below.

	Version 1 (Roberta Flack)	Version 2 (Fugees)
Instrumentation		
Vocals / Backing vocals		
Texture		
Dynamics		
Style		
Form		

Research Assignments

1 Three main strands run through 1990s pop music: rock and indie, dance, and manufactured pop.
   (a) Describe the general and musical characteristics of each strand.
   (b) Choose three bands from the following list – one for each category. Write a paragraph about each band, outlining the features of their style.
      Happy Mondays   The Prodigy   Spice Girls
      Primal Scream   Orbital   Take That
   (c) Describe an album or song by each band, showing in what way it is representative of the strand it belongs to.

2 Björk's style has often been described as eclectic and experimental. Give a brief outline of her career from her early influences to her most recent recordings to illustrate this eclecticism.

3 Take three of the following dance music styles and complete a table like the one below.
   (a) house
   (b) techno
   (c) trip-hop
   (d) jungle / drum 'n' bass
   (e) hardcore
   (f) big beat

Dance style	Tempo (bpm)	Musical characteristics	Example – name a track and an artist or band

The History of Recording

Quick Questions

Background information in *Pop Music: the Text Book* pages 107–114.

1 How did Edison's phonograph work?

2 When were microphones first used in recording studios?
  (a) 1915
  (b) 1925
  (c) 1945
  What impact did the microphone have on musical styles when it first appeared?

3 In 1927 the first successful sound film appeared.
  (a) What was it called?
  (b) What was the sound recorded on?

4 When magnetic tape was first invented, what advantages did it have over the direct recording process?

5 What do you understand by the term musique concrète?

Essays

1 (a) Describe three ways in which pop music has influenced the development of music technology.
  (b) Describe three ways in which music technology has influenced the development of pop music

2 Give a brief description of
  (a) the phonograph
  (b) the graphophone
  (c) the gramophone
  Why was the gramophone ultimately the most successful of the three?

3 Outline the contribution of the following to the development of the recording industry
  (a) Bing Crosby
  (b) Les Paul
  (c) Phil Spector
  (d) George Martin

4 What is the difference between analogue and digital recording? Describe some of the advantages and disadvantages of both processes.

5 *Loveless* by My Bloody Valentine famously took nearly two years to record. How are recording techniques used creatively on this album?

Listening Questions

1 Listen to 'West End blues' played by Louis Armstrong and his Hot Five. This track was recorded in 1928. Describe two qualities present in the recording that indicate that it was recorded then rather than nowadays.

2 Listen to 'That's all right' as recorded by Elvis Presley in 1954.
  (a) Identify two musical features that are typical of 1950s music.
  (b) Describe two qualities present in the recording which indicate that it was recorded in the 1950s rather than the present day.

3 Listen to 'River deep – mountain high' by Ike and Tina Turner. Describe the musical and production features that are typical of Phil Spector's output.

4 Compare the sound and production of 'New rose' by the Damned and 'Anarchy in the UK' by the Sex Pistols.

5 Choose any track from Pink Floyd's *Dark Side of the Moon* and compare it with any 1970s punk track.
  (a) Show how recording techniques are used to enhance the lush production of the Pink Floyd track.
  (b) Show how recording techniques are used to enhance the low-budget, live, immediate feel of the punk track.

6 George Martin used many imaginative production skills on the Beatles recordings. Choose one track from *Sergeant Pepper's Lonely Hearts Club Band* or from the *White Album* and describe some of the techniques and effects used.

7 Listen to 'Two tribes' by Frankie Goes to Hollywood. In what ways is this a typical Trevor Horn production?

8 'It's a sin' was recorded by the Pet Shop Boys in 1987. Describe some of the qualities present in the music and the recording which indicate that it is a 1980s production rather than one from the 1950s.

9 Briefly describe three technological resources that you can hear in the Pulp song 'Common people'.

Research Assignment

1 Choose three different recordings. The first should be pre-1940, the second from the 1960s or 1970s, and the third post-2000. For each of these recordings:
  (a) Describe the recording techniques that would have been used at the time.
  (b) Describe the means of playback available at the time.
  (c) Listen to the recording and give three pieces of musical evidence and three pieces of technological evidence which indicate roughly when it was recorded.

Acoustic Instruments

Quick Questions

1 Describe, as if to a non-guitarist, what is meant by:
(a) a capo (b) hammer-on (c) pull-off

2 How do the soundboard and soundhole of a guitar help to produce the sound?

3 Explain what you understand by the terms
(a) backbeat (b) pulse
Which type of drum usually creates the backbeat?

4 Explain to a non-drummer the difference between a roll and a paradiddle.

5 What is the difference between a hi-hat and a ride cymbal?

6 What is a rim shot?

Essays

1 What are the main components of a drum kit? Describe some of the ways in which a kit is played.

2 Name two drummers with contrasting styles. How would you describe and assess their playing?

Listening Questions

1 Listen to 'Black and tan fantasy' by Duke Ellington. Name three jazz techniques found in the brass solos.

2 Listen to 'Tupelo honey' by Van Morrison.
Two wind instruments are used on this recording. Name them, and describe where and how they are used in the song.
Which of these is a transposing instrument?

3 Listen to 'Trenchtown rock' by Bob Marley and the Wailers.
On which beats of the bar does the bass drum play?
How is the snare drum used?

Research Assignment

1 Describe the following playing techniques which would be used by instruments in the horn section:
(a) flutter tonguing (b) growl (c) bend (d) vibrato
Find and discuss recorded examples of each.

Electronic Instruments

Quick Questions

Background information in *Pop Music: the Text Book* pages 115–122.

1 Describe the effects produced by each of the following guitar pedals:
 (a) Wah-wah pedal (c) Whammy pedal
 (b) Echo pedal (d) Fuzzbox

2 What are the main differences between rhythm and lead guitar playing?

3 Outline the main differences in sound production between an acoustic guitar and a solid-body electric guitar.

4 Explain what is meant by flanging and phasing.

5 What do you understand by the terms:
 (a) monophonic
 (b) polyphonic

6 What is a Mellotron and how does it work?

7 What is a MIDI controller?

8 Early synthesizers were mainly analogue and monophonic. Explain what is meant by these terms.

Essays

1 Of all the instruments used in pop music, why do you think the electric guitar came to have such an important role?

2 Describe three ways in which a guitar sound can be distorted. In each case give an example of a track in which this effect can be heard. Discuss the expressive effects that can be achieved through use of distortion.

3 What does a guitar amplifier do? Outline some of the developments in the manufacture of guitar amplifiers from the 1940s to the 1970s.

4 What was so innovative about Jimi Hendrix's style in comparison to what had come before? Outline his approach to guitar playing with reference to playing techniques, improvisation, amplification, sound effects and live performance. Your answer should refer to at least two songs in some detail.

5 How have synthesizers helped to change styles of pop music?

6 Give a brief history of the development of the turntable as a musical instrument.

Listening Questions

1 Listen to 'Star spangled banner' as played by Jimi Hendrix, and describe some of the playing techniques that he uses.

2 Describe some of the guitar-playing techniques used by Ed Van Halen on 'Eruption' or any other of his songs.

3 Listen to 'Nutbush city limits' by Ike and Tina Turner. Below are the names of five guitar effects pedals. Which of them can be heard in this song and where?
   (a) fuzz
   (b) overdrive
   (c) wah-wah
   (d) tremolo
   (e) delay

   Which of the following best describes what the lead rhythm guitar plays at the beginning of this track?
   (a) fill
   (b) riff
   (c) break
   (d) lick

4 Listen to *Switched On Bach* recorded by Walter Carlos. Choose one of the tracks and compare it with the original keyboard or orchestral version.
   (a) What are the similarities and differences?
   (b) Which do you prefer? Give two musical reasons for your choice.
   (c) This album was recorded on a Moog. Describe briefly how a Moog works.

Research Assignments

1 Leon Thérémin and Maurice Martenot both invented instruments that are named after them. Write about:
   (a) the ondes martenot
   (b) the thérémin

   Describe the sounds these instruments can make, the manner of sound-production, and the way in which they are played. Refer to pieces of music which use them.

2 (a) Where was the original Dr Who theme recorded?
   (b) Why do you think it caused such a stir when it was first heard?
   (c) The VCS3 was used extensively on this recording. Describe briefly how a VCS3 works.

3 Describe the function of each of the four core elements of the synthesizer.
   (a) Oscillator
   (b) Filter
   (c) Envelope
   (d) Modulation

Digital Technology

Quick Questions

Background information in *Pop Music: the Text Book* pages 123–129.

1 What is MIDI an abbreviation for?

2 How did the introduction of MIDI in the 1980s help lead to house music?

3 What is a TR909? Explain why it is often credited with the birth of house music.

Essays

1 Outline some of the creative possibilities which MIDI opened up for musicians when it was introduced.

2 How are samplers typically used in drum 'n' bass music? Refer to any well-known dance track in your answer.

3 Compare the capabilities of either Logic Audio or Cubase Audio with the Sibelius software package.

4 How do sample rate and bit resolution help to determine the quality of a sample?

5 When were the first samplers introduced and what was their function? How have samplers developed since then?

6 Outline some of the ways in which twenty-first-century computers can be used to produce pop music.

7 'Dance music would not exist without digital technology.' Discuss.

8 Explain the importance of the Roland TB303 and TR909 in the history of dance music.

Listening Questions

1 Describe Jim Steinman's production on 'This corrosion' by the Sisters of Mercy.

2 Listen to 'Heartbreak Hotel' by Elvis Presley. An echo effect is used in this song. How could a similar effect be produced using digital technology?

3 Listen to 'Being boiled' or another track by the Human League. How has music technology been used to enhance and realize this song?

4 Describe how samples are used on either 'Pump up the volume' by M/A/R/R/S or 'Theme from S'Express' by S'Express.

Style and Structure

Quick Questions

Background information in *Pop Music: the Text Book* pages 133–158.

1 What is a chord?

2 If A is the tonic chord, which chord is the dominant?

3 If G is the dominant chord, which chord is the subdominant?

4 In the key of C, which are chords I, IV and V?

5 What is a 7th chord?

6 What is a blue note?

7 Describe the main characteristics of the blues.

8 What is the standard lyric structure of a blues song?

9 Complete the lyrics for a verse of the blues using the following first line:

I'm so lonely I don't know what to do

10 Give a name for:
- a) an opening section
- b) a closing section

11 What do you understand by the term 'stop time'?

12

What is the name for this type of bass line?
Which bars form the turnaround?
What is the function of a turnaround?

13 Explain what you understand by the Bo Diddley beat. Name any song you know which uses the Bo Diddley beat.

14 How does a typical reggae rhythm differ from a typical disco rhythm?

15 What is a power chord? Name a style of music that often uses power chords.

16 What is the term used when offbeats are accented?

17 What does bpm stand for?

18 Name two differences between a typical verse and a typical chorus.

19 Which instruments (apart from drums and guitar) are commonly heard in soul music?

20 Call and response is often used in soul music. Explain what it means.

21 Describe these different vocal styles
   a) punk
   b) rap
   c) ballad

22 Give another name for a short, catchy melodic or rhythmic idea. Give an example from any well-known pop song.

23 Describe two characteristics of a riff.

24 What are the distinctive features of:
   (a) Acid House
   (b) Filtered House
   (c) Jungle

Essays

1 Identify some of the musical hallmarks of rock 'n' roll.

2 Give a brief description of 32-bar song form.

Research Assignments

1 Take three pop songs in verse-and-chorus form and show through analysis how they are variants on the original A A B A 32-bar form.

2 Dance music of the 1980s moved away from the traditional pop template of the verse/chorus form. Describe the ways in which dance tracks were usually structured, using appropriate musical vocabulary. Include a detailed analysis of at least one song in your answer.

Listening Questions

The questions included here are mostly about songs featured in detail in the Style and Structure chapter in *Pop Music: the Text Book*. Many more listening questions are included under their respective decades. See sections starting on pages 16, 20, 22, 25, 28, 31.

1 Listen to 'Rock around the clock' by Bill Haley and the Comets.

How is tension built up in the intro? What makes it so striking?

Explain what you understand by the following terms
(a) turnaround
(b) riff

Which of the following shapes best represents the turnaround at the end of the song?

a) 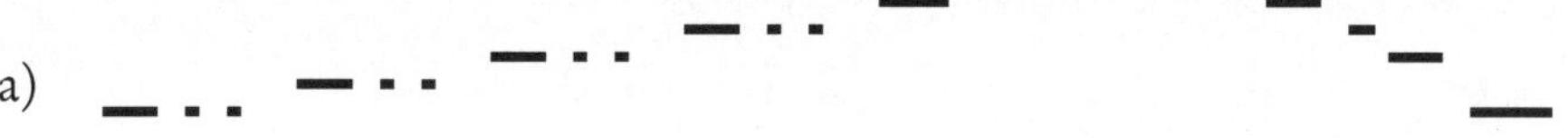

b) 

c)

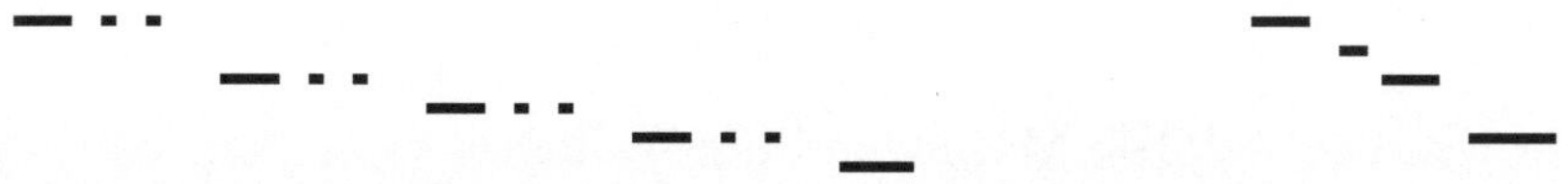

2 Listen to 'Maybe baby' by Buddy Holly and the Crickets. The form of this song is:

Intro – Verse 1 – Verse 2 – Middle eight – Verse 1 (repeat) –
Instrumental based on verse – Middle eight – Verse 1 (repeat) – Ending

What is another way of expressing this structure using letternames – A, B etc.?
The backing vocals use close harmony. What is close harmony?
How is contrast achieved in the middle eight?

3 Listen to 'I want to hold your hand' by the Beatles.

Describe how three of the following are varied in the middle eight:
(a) vocals
(b) drum part
(c) lyrics
(d) harmony

4 Listen to 'Waterloo sunset' by the Kinks.

Which sentence best describes the bass guitar line in the opening of this song
- (a) It ascends in stepwise movement
- (b) It descends in stepwise movement
- (c) It is a descending chromatic scale

Which of the following is the musical form of the verse:
- (a) AABB
- (b) AAAB
- (c) AABA

Explain what you understand by the following terms:
- (a) middle eight
- (b) drum fill
- (c) guitar lick

Identify where each of them can be found in 'Waterloo sunset'.

Write a sentence to describe what the backing vocals do in this song.

5 Listen to 'You've got a friend' by James Taylor. This record is in the American singer-songwriter tradition. What are some of the features of this style as heard in this song?

Name two other American singer-songwriters of the 1970s.

6 Listen to 'Soul man' by Sam and Dave.
What gives this song the typical Atlantic/Stax soul sound?
How many verses are there in this verse-and-chorus song?
Where does the middle eight appear?
Where does the song change key?

7 Listen to any song by Bob Marley. Identify three features of the song that are typical of reggae.

8 Listen to 'Trenchtown rock' by Bob Marley and the Wailers.
What is the tempo?
How many beats are there in a bar?
Explain what you understand by the term improvisation. Where can improvisation be heard in this song?

This song is in verse-and-chorus form with two long middle sections. Which of the following statements is true?
- (a) The verse and chorus are in the minor and the middle sections use major chords.
- (b) The verse and chorus are in the major and the middle sections use minor chords.
- (c) The verse, chorus and the middle section are all in the major.

Where does the material for the outro come from?

9 Listen to 'Get up (I feel like being a) sex machine' by James Brown.

This song is groove-based. Explain what you understand by this term.

Explain what you understand by the following:
(a) horn stabs
(b) piano riff

Which of the following statements is true?
(a) The song uses a repeated chord progression.
(b) The song is based on the 12-bar blues.
(c) The song uses only two chords.

10 Listen to 'Disco inferno' by the Trammps.
Name three elements of 'Disco inferno' that are typical of disco music.
Name two instruments that you can hear apart from bass and drums.
What makes the intro of this song so striking?
This song is groove-based. Explain what you understand by the term 'groove'.
Which appears first, the verse or the chorus?

Which one of the following statements is true of the harmony?
(a) Both the verse and the chorus are based on a descending chord sequence.
(b) The verse is based on one minor chord and the chorus uses major chords.
(c) The chorus is based on one major chord and the verse uses minor chords.

11 Listen to 'Holidays in the sun' by the Sex Pistols. Outline some of the musical characteristics of punk that you can hear in this song. Include reference to:
(a) vocal style
(b) instrumentation
(c) lyrics
(d) tempo
(e) guitar solo
(f) texture

12 Listen to 'Smells like teen spirit' by Nirvana.

How is excitement generated in the intro?

Which of the following is the rhythm of the opening riff?
(The crossed noteheads indicate damped notes.)

a) 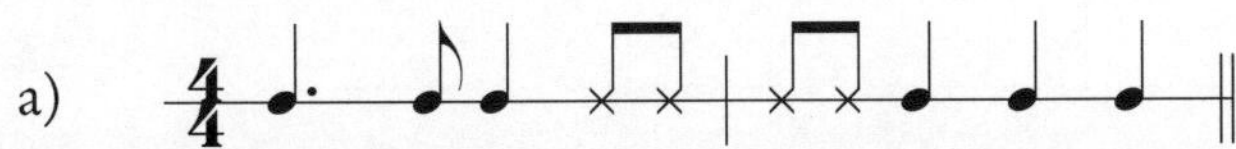

b) 

c) 

Describe how dynamics are used in the verse and the chorus.

Where does the material for the guitar solo come from?

13 Listen to 'Bring the noise' by Public Enemy.
   There are two vocalists. What does the second rapper add to the song?
   How is this song typical of 1980s hip-hop?

14 Listen to 'Independent women Pt 1' by Destiny's Child.
   Describe the key features of R&B that you can hear.
   How does the music of the chorus differ and develop each time it is heard?
   Explain what you understand by call and response. Describe how this feature is used in the song.
   Describe the vocals in the middle eight (the section before the final chorus).

15 Describe the main musical elements of big beat as used in any of the tracks on *Better Living through Chemistry* by Fatboy Slim.

16 Listen to 'Renegade master' by Fatboy Slim. This track is mostly on the chord of C. How does Fatboy Slim maintain the interest in the song?

17 Listen to 'Access' by DJ Misjah and DJ Tim.
   How would you describe the bass drum pattern?
   Which instrument has the main pulse?
   Which instrument does the mix in start with?
   The main section features a pedal note.
      (a) What is a pedal note?
      (b) What sound is used for the pedal note?
   Where is the climax of this track?
   How is the climax achieved?
   What is the only instrument playing in the mix out?

18 Take any dance track that you know, and use CD timings to show where the various sections are. Give timings also for any other points of interest, e.g. use of samples, scratching, breaks, etc.

	CD TIMINGS e.g. 1:32 (1 minute 32 seconds)
Mix in	
Main section	
Breakdown	
Reprise of main section	
Mix out	

The Music Business

Quick Questions

Background information in *Pop Music: the Text Book* pages 159–174.

1 How does a mechanical royalty differ from a performance royalty?

2 What is a playlist?

3 What are the main responsibilities of a tour manager?

Essays

1 What do you need to do to put on a successful gig?

2 What are the advantages and disadvantages in signing up to:
 (a) a major label
 (b) an indie label

3 What is copyright? What types of copyright are there? Why is copyright so important in today's music industry?

4 Why is it important for a performance act to have a manager? What are the principal roles that managers undertake for their acts?

5 What are the most important things to remember when marketing a new band?

6 Why are lawyers so important in the music business?

Research Assignments

1 Who, apart from the musicians, would you expect to find on the payroll when a successful band is on tour? Take three of these jobs and outline their contribution to the tour.

2 At most big-budget recording sessions you would expect to find a producer, an engineer, an assistant engineer and a studio manager. Describe what each of them would contribute to the recording process.

3 Outline the process a CD goes through from the end of the recording session until it arrives in the shops.

4 Outline some of the copyright issues concerning the use of sampling.

5 What is A&R? Describe some of the functions that an A&R person undertakes.

6 How significant is the development of new electronic distribution channels in the production of music? Discuss some of the main developments in this field.

Links with Courses and Examinations

The questions and answers in this book have been written with a range of examination boards in mind. For instance BTEC students and lecturers will find the chapters on Context and the Music Business particularly relevant to their courses. In different ways all of the chapters will be useful to students on all courses, although some chapters will be more relevant than others. The table below picks out some of the more obvious links.

	Coping with Exam Questions	Context and History							Instruments and Technology					
		Context	Origins	1950s	1960s	1970s	1980s	1990s	History of Recording	Acoustic Instruments	Electronic Instruments	Digital Technology	**Style and Structure**	**The Music Business**
Edexcel GCSE Music	✓	✓	✓		✓		✓	✓		✓	✓		✓	
AQA GCSE Music	✓	✓			✓	✓	✓	✓		✓	✓		✓	
OCR GCSE Music	✓	✓				✓	✓	✓		✓			✓	
Edexcel AS/A2 GCE Music	✓	✓	✓	✓	✓	✓	✓	✓			✓		✓	
Edexcel AS/A2 GCE Music Technology	✓	✓	✓	✓	✓	✓	✓	✓	✓		✓	✓	✓	
Rockschool	✓	✓	✓	✓	✓	✓	✓	✓		✓	✓		✓	✓
BTEC First Diploma Performing Arts (Music)	✓	✓							✓		✓	✓	✓	✓
BTEC National Diploma Music Technology	✓	✓							✓		✓	✓	✓	✓
BTEC National Diploma Music Practice	✓	✓											✓	✓
BTEC Higher National Diploma Music Production	✓	✓							✓		✓	✓	✓	✓
BTEC Higher National Diploma Music Performance	✓	✓											✓	✓
BA Music Technology	✓	✓							✓		✓	✓	✓	✓
BA Popular Music	✓	✓											✓	✓

Answers to Quick Questions

This question-book is closely linked to *Pop Music: the Text Book*, and many of the answers to factual questions can be found there – as well as an overview of the historical and stylistic dimensions, which may help set more subjectively-based answers in a wider perspective. Where exact answers are not possible we have identified probable significant points or aspects.

Origins (page 16)

1 *Rhythmic features* Syncopation, polyrhythms, cross rhythms, ostinati (repeated patterns), rhythmic complexity.
Aspects carried over Importance of rhythm, percussion, syncopation; use of call and response, or of improvisation; association with dance, or with work; music not usually notated.

2 Originally associated with slavery, worksongs were sung rhythmically in time with the task. Songs used call and response: one member of the gang would lead the singing with the others coming in after him. The mid-nineteenth century was an important age for the worksong: there was a huge demand for labour to construct new transport systems. Worksongs continued to be sung in the twentieth century, particularly by workgangs in the southern gaols.

3 Minstrel songs and shows, burlesque, vaudeville

4 (a) *Call and response* This is where a soloist sings or plays a phrase to which a larger group responds with an answering phrase.
(b) *Styles in which call and response can be found* worksongs, blues, gospel, soul, R&B

5 (a) *Talking drums* African drums that are used to convey messages. The drums are made to play at different pitches by pressing the skin. In this way pitches of speech are imitated.
(b) *Oral tradition* Where music is passed on by word of mouth rather than written down.
(c) *Worksong* See Q2 above.

1950s (page 19)

1 Sentimental ballads, novelty songs, songs from musicals, Tin Pan Alley songs

2 Teenage culture, girls, cars (automobiles), love songs, dancing, drive-in movies, having fun

3 (a) *Major record labels* Answers could include RCA, Columbia, Capitol, Decca, MGM, Mercury.
(b) *Independents* Answers could include Sun, Imperial, Specialty, Chess, Atlantic, King, Liberty.

4 *Skiffle* Mid-50s British style similar to early rock 'n' roll, originated from 'trad' jazz bands and with a repertoire based on folk-blues and other American folk styles.
Which instruments gave characteristic sound? guitar, double bass, washboard, sometimes banjo

5 *Bo Diddley beat* (a)

1960s (page 21)

1 (a) *Brill Building* Early 60s pop 'hit factory': songwriters or songwriting teams such as Neil Sedaka, Goffin/King, Mann/Weil.
(b) *Greenwich Village* Urban folk movement particularly associated with Woody Guthrie and Bob Dylan.
(c) *Jamaica* ska, rocksteady, reggae

2 *Americans who influenced British R&B* Chuck Berry, Little Richard, Fats Domino, Muddy Waters, Howlin' Wolf, Elmore James, Little Walter, Buddy Guy, Elvis Presley, Ray Charles, Jimmy Reed, John Lee Hooker

3 *Prince Buster* A big figure on the Jamaican sound system scene in the 1960s. His most famous hit was the ska song 'Al Capone'.

4 A2, B1, C4, D3

5 *Phil Spector* Successful record producer whose distinctive sound was called the 'wall of sound'. This rich texture used echo, tape loops, multi-layering and a powerful backbeat. Famously found in hits by Ronettes, Crystals, Righteous Bros, Ike and Tina Turner.

1970s (page 24)

1 *Two Tone* ska
Trojan Records reggae
Alternative Tentacles US hardcore

2 *Concept album* An album with a theme or story running through it. Examples from the 70s could include *Dark Side of the Moon* (Pink Floyd), *Tales from Topographic Oceans* (Yes), *Bat Out of Hell* (Meatloaf).
Prog rock An album-based style with large-scale compositions and extended solos (usually guitar). Many albums were concept-based, telling epic stories or with over-arching themes. Sometimes looked beyond the boundaries of rock music, coupling wild poetic lyrics with synthesizers, electronics, jazz, psychedelia, classical music. Examples might include King Crimson, Emerson Lake and Palmer, Jethro Tull, Traffic, Yes, Genesis.
Guitar hero Virtuosic player, often central focus of a band. Extended guitar solos, long improvisations, electronic effects. Examples could include Jimi Hendrix, Eric Clapton, Jimmy Page, Peter Green.

3 *Dub recording* Popular in 1970s reggae. Techniques included changing volume levels in the mix, bringing instruments up and dropping them out, adding reverb and echo effects.
Sound system Originally found in Jamaica, sound systems used home-made box speakers to play the latest records. The term came to refer to the combination of disc jockey and equipment. Later gave rise to offshoots such as dub, toasting or rapping, scratching and dance music. Today sound systems use huge banks of speakers.
Toasting Rhythmic, rhyming speech over reggae music. As early as the 1950s, DJs would talk/toast over the sounds produced on sound systems. Toasting was later to have a bearing on the rise of rap in the US.

4 *Saturday Night Fever* disco; *The Harder They Come* reggae; *The Great Rock 'n' Roll Swindle* punk; *Spinal Tap* heavy metal

5 Originating in Philadelphia, notable for lavish productions featuring strings and soulful vocals. Artists include Jerry Butler, O'Jays, Delfonics, Stylistics.

6 Starting and ending with a heartbeat, *The Dark Side of the Moon* is a single extended piece rather than a collection of songs. The theme running throughout is the dark side of contemporary life.

1980s (page 27)

1 *Breaks* One instrument (or singer) continues while all others stop. Usually just one or two bars long.
Breakdancing Athletic dancing incorporating martial arts moves and gymnastics as well as head- and back-spinning. So called because dancers hit the floor during the extended break sections played by the DJs.

2 *Tapping* A technique whereby a guitarist plays notes by tapping the neck with the right hand, enabling very fast playing.
Divebombing A guitar technique which allows drastic changes of pitch obtained via the locking tremolo arm.

3 *Balearic beat* Played by DJs in clubs in Ibiza in the 1980s, including such disparate artists as U2, Penguin Café Orchestra and Nitzer Ebb, alongside house and techno. The mixing together of different genres became known as the 'Balearic sound' or 'Balearic beat'.
Where heard Originally Ibiza, later imported to the UK.

4 *Rough Trade* Indie groups such as the Fall
Sugarhill Records rap *Def Jam* rap

5 *Four-on-the-floor* The bass drum plays on each beat of the bar. Associated with disco.

6 'House' started in the Warehouse club in Chicago, where DJ Frankie Knuckles began to mix records on the dance floor using a reel-to-reel tape recorder and a drum machine. The four-on-the-floor bass drum, syncopated hi-hats and soulful vocals can all be traced back to disco.

7 'Garage' is named after a New York club called the Paradise Garage.

8 Black clothes, horror and occult literature (especially vampire literature, e.g. *Dracula*).

9 Faster, more raw and hard-edged, featuring extreme changes of tempo, and dense, doubled-tracked guitars.

10 *Musical* Rhythmic recitation using rhyming. Often complex rhythms. Often two rappers work in rhythmic counterpoint. Uses DJ-ing and remixing where existing recordings are manipulated and combined.
Non-musical US urban black culture, graffiti art, breakdancing

1990s (page 30)

1 *Two styles combined to create bhangra.* Traditional Pakistani folk songs and Western pop music.

2 *Musical features of ambient or chill-out music* Soft, slowly-evolving musical landscapes with no strong pulse or beat. 'Ambient' means surrounding, and is used for things which are all around. 'Chill-out' rooms appeared in clubs from the early 1990s; clubbers would take time out from dancing to relax on cushions and listen to soft music.

3 *Rap battle* A contest where rappers improvise, trying to better each other's raps.

4 *TB303* A transistor bass designed as a substitute bass player and including a simple sequencer. Used in many songs including Fatboy Slim's 'Everybody needs a 303' and Phuture's 'Acid trax'.

5 (a) *mix in* The opening section of a dance track, where the DJ mixes the track in over the end of the previous one.
(b) *mix out* The closing section of a dance track, where the DJ begins to mix in the next track.
(c) *breakdown* The section of a dance track where sounds drop out in order to create tension as they build up again and maintain the excitement.
All these terms are associated with dance music.

The History of Recording (page 33)

1 Edison spoke into the horn of a hand-cranked machine which captured the vibrations of his voice by means of a diaphragm with a needle attached. The needle recorded the vibrations by indenting them onto a continuously grooved, revolving metal cylinder wrapped in tin foil. The sound could then be played back.

2 *Microphones first used in recording studios* (b) 1925.
What impact on musical styles Microphones helped the voice to be heard over the jazz bands and swing orchestras. They also allowed singers to sing softly, 'crooning', with the microphone held close to the singer's mouth. Increased frequency range meant that the string bass could be more easily heard, replacing the tuba.

3 *The Jazz Singer*, recorded on gramophone records

4 *Advantages of magnetic tape* Allowed editing. Seamless splice editing allowed producers to use the best material from a number of takes.

5 *Musique concrète* Music based on environmental or everyday sounds, recorded and then transformed by, for example, playing backwards, speeding up, slowing down, splicing, and looping. Pioneered by Pierre Schaeffer in the 1940s.

Acoustic Instruments (page 35)

1 (a) *Capo* A clamp, used on different frets of a guitar to change the pitch of the open strings.
(b) *Hammer-on* Allows two notes to be played for every one picked by the RH. The first note is played in the usual manner, the second (a higher note on the same string) by 'hammering on' just behind the fret with one of the free fingers of the LH. The hammer-on slurs the two notes together.
(c) *Pull-off* Reverse of hammer-on: the LH finger pressing the string down is 'pulled off', thereby plucking another (lower) note. This technique also slurs the notes together.

2 When the strings vibrate in an acoustic guitar, the vibrations travel through the saddle to the bridge to the soundboard. The body of the guitar forms a hollow soundbox that amplifies the vibrations of the soundboard.

3 (a) *Backbeat* The rhythmic emphasis on beats 2 and 4 within a four-beat bar.
(b) *Pulse* The underlying beat.
Usual drum for backbeat Snare (with bass drum often on beats 1 and 3).

4 Both are types of drum roll. The difference lies in how hands are alternated. A roll uses double strokes: RRLLRRLL. A paradiddle is more complex: RLRRLRLL.

5 *Hi-hat* Two cymbals mounted together on a single stand, controlled by a foot pedal so that they can be played open or closed, or clashed together using the pedal.
Ride cymbal Biggest cymbal in a drum kit, used to maintain a rhythm rather than provide accents.

6 *Rim shot* The drummer strikes the head and the rim (of the snare drum) at the same time, giving a punchy accent. A 'rim click' is similar but gentler: striking the rim *instead* of the head, typically using the butt end of the stick while the tip rests against the drumhead.

Electronic Instruments (page 36)

1 (a) *Wah-wah* Varies treble/bass balance. So called because it can emulate the sound of crying.
(b) *Echo* Repeats a sound, often softer or fading away.
(c) *Whammy* Enables the guitarist to bend the pitch of the instrument up or down two octaves, or alternatively to play a self-harmonizing line.
(d) *Fuzzbox* Distorts, creating a fuzzy sound.

2 The rhythm guitar is part of the underlying rhythm section while the lead guitar is a solo voice. Most rhythm guitar playing centres on chords (harmony), whereas the lead guitar plays mostly a single line (melody).

3 In both types of guitar the sound is produced by a vibrating string. In an acoustic guitar, the vibrations travel through the saddle to the bridge to the soundboard. The body of the guitar forms a hollow soundbox that amplifies the vibrations of the soundboard. In an electric guitar, the vibration of the string is picked up by a magnetic pickup, which sends an electronic signal to an amplifier. The amplifier takes the signal and makes it audible by boosting it enough to drive a speaker.

4 A flanger works by mixing the original sound with a very slightly delayed version, resulting in a whooshing, jet-like effect. Phasing is a similar effect, producing a gentler, sweeping sound.

5 (a) *monophonic* one sound: a single melodic line; an instrument that can only play single notes
(b) *polyphonic* many sounds: two or more melodic lines blended together; an instrument that can play several notes simultaneously

6 *Mellotron* An early sample player, using tape loops. Each key set a length of tape in motion, playing back whatever was recorded on the tape. It was a complicated instrument to master: the left-hand keyboard played different rhythms and accompaniments, while the right-hand keyboard played lead-lines or chords.

7 *MIDI controller* An electronic instrument based on an existing acoustic model but using MIDI technology.

8 *Analogue* The recorded signal is stored in patterns which correspond with (are analogous to) the waveforms of the original sound.
Monophonic Literally 'one sound'. Monophonic synthesizers can only play one note at a time.

Digital Technology (page 38)

1 Musical Instrument Digital Interface

2 MIDI enabled one musician to control many different electronic instruments, with ease and affordably. The short, repeating patterns of house music were facilitated, even encouraged, by the technology available, which initially did not allow long patterns to be programmed.

3 The TR909 drum machine was produced by Roland in 1983, using synthesized drum sounds, including a powerful bass drum, aggressive snare drum and hard metallic hi-hats. It has been used on many house records, and also on trance and techno tracks.

Style and Structure (page 39)

1 The simultaneous sounding of two or more notes.

2 *Dominant of A* E

3 *Subdominant of G* C

4 C, F and G

5 A 7th chord includes the 7th note above its root as well as the 3rd and the 5th.

6 Compared with the major scale, blue notes are flattened – usually the 3rd, 5th or 7th. They may be flattened by a semitone or 'bent' by a smaller interval.

7 12-bar chord structure based on I, IV and V. Three line verse with AAB structure. Use of

blue notes, note-bending. Sometimes in slow tempo, with sad or troubled lyrics.

8 AAB. The text of the second phrase is usually a repeat of the first; then the third phrase uses different words – usually an advance or a response to what came before.

10 (a) *Opening section* Intro
(b) *Closing section* Outro or coda

11 *Stop time* The accompaniment is reduced to a stab on the first beat of each bar, or similar short figure, leaving the singer or instrumentalist unaccompanied for a short passage.

12 *Type of bass line* walking bass
Turnaround bars 11 and 12
Function of a turnaround Provides a smooth transition into the next section.

13 *Bo Diddley beat* Distinctive rhythmic pattern much used by Bo Diddley. Sometime known as 'shave and a haircut, two bits' because these words match the rhythm of the phrase. 'Bo Diddley' by Bo Diddley is the classic example. Other examples include 'Not fade away' (Buddy Holly, or version by Rolling Stones), 'Magic bus' (the Who), 'She's the one' (Bruce Springsteen).

14 *Reggae rhythm* Emphasis on the offbeat – beats 2 and 4 of the bar.
Disco Four-on-the-floor beat emphasizes all four beats of the bar.

15 *Power chord* Powerful, heavy guitar chord, frequently played with distortion, often containing only the root and fifth. Often found in heavy metal.

16 *Offbeats accented* syncopation

17 beats per minute

18 *Verse* Usually has different words with each repetition.
Chorus Normally has the same words each time. Often contains the title words of the song. Normally the 'catchiest' part of the song.

19 Often strings and a horn section.

20 *Call and response* A soloist sings or plays a phrase to which a larger group responds with an answering phrase.

21 (a) *Punk* Fast, energetic, declamatory – a sneering recitative half way between speaking (or shouting) and singing. Often uses vernacular accent.
(b) *Rap* Rhythmical, rhyming, semi-spoken recitation, often with spoken ad libs.
(c) *Ballad* Slow, usually romantic, melodic, expressive.

22 A hook

23 *Riff* A short, repeated melodic pattern, often in the bass, often forming the background to a solo or vocal line. Usually 2–4 bars long.

24 (a) *Acid House* House music features four-on-the-floor bass drum and off-beat hi-hat patterns and is sample-oriented. As implied by its name and its association with the drug ecstasy, acid house has a psychedelic, funky feel with jerky synth rhythms.
(b) *Filtered House* A style of house music which made much use of 1970s disco sounds, looped and filtered. Sometimes whole sections were filtered.
(c) *Jungle* Uses speeded-up hip-hop breaks, and often consists of little other than a drum loop and a heavy bass-line. Tempo generally around 170 bpm.

The Music Business (page 45)

1 *Mechanical royalties* Generated from the recording of music, and the reproduction of recordings, whether on CDs, DVDs, videos or any other format, or for distribution online. Administered in the UK through MCPS.
Performance royalties Due whenever copyright music, live or recorded, is broadcast or played in public. Administered in the UK through PRS.

2 *Playlist* List of records to be played regularly by a radio station.

3 *Tour manager* Responsible for organizing and overseeing transport, accommodation, staff, budget and itinerary for a tour, and for making sure the band/artist is in the right place at the right time.

Answers to Listening Questions

Many of the recordings are included in Peters Edition anthologies (*The New Anthology of Music*, *The GCSE Anthology of Music*, *The AQA GCSE Anthology of Music*), together with printed transcriptions or charts. Many are mentioned in *Pop Music: the Text Book*; the Style and Structure chapter includes general stylistic guidelines as well as analytical charts of 16 songs in a range of styles.

Where exact answers are not possible, probable significant points or aspects are identified. Where there is an open choice of track/song, the question is usually of a standard type; general advice on answering such questions is contained in 'Exam Tips' (pages 8–9).

Origins (page 16)

1 **Scott Joplin**
- (a) *Tempo* probably moderate/medium or quite slow
- (b) *Beats per bar* four
- (c) *LH rhythm* regular march-like
- (d) *RH rhythm* syncopated, more complex than LH
- (e) *How many themes* Usually four or more. 'The entertainer' and 'Maple Leaf rag' both have four.

2 **'West End blues'**
- (a) *Structure* 12-bar blues, five times through ('choruses' or 'verses') with intro and coda
- (b) *Front line* trumpet, clarinet, trombone
- (c) *Rhythm section* piano, banjo, drums/percussion

3 (NB choose a recording where the key and chords can be readily identified.)

4 **'Black and tan fantasy'**
- (a) *Swung rhythm* Division of the beat into pairs of notes where the first note is longer than the second. Approximates to:

- (b) *Syncopation* Off-beat notes are accented.
- (c) *Substitution chords* A complex or chromatic chord replaces a simple chord (usually with the same tonal function).

Elements used in pop music Use of drums and horn section, 12-bar blues chord sequence and structure, syncopation, blue notes, swung rhythm, improvisation.

Shortcomings in recording techniques 78s were restricted in duration (compare CDs). Stereo technology not yet invented, so 1920s recordings are in mono. Balance was achieved by placement of the musicians in relation to the microphone; this often resulted in poor balance, with some instruments sounding distant or poorly focused. Nowadays multitrack recording allows balance to be manipulated in the mix. Early recordings had a limited frequency range.

Variety added to the 12-bar blues structure Use of different soloists in each verse (trumpet, piano, trombone), each with a different style. Saxophone solo uses a different chord sequence. Song ends with a quotation from Chopin's funeral march.

5 **'Summertime'**
- (a) *Chromatic scale* All the intervals are semitones.
- (b) *Chromatic harmony* Coloured with altered or added notes, many outside the scale of the key.

Form of verse ABAB

6 **'Summertime'**

Why so popular Highly distinctive, memorable melody (even though built from simple elements, and quite easy to sing), stands out from other songs of this period. Words simple but effective, combining with melody and rich chromatic harmonies to make an intense mood. Chord sequence also distinctive, well suited to varied arrangements or jazz improvisation.

(See model answer for comparison questions on pages 11–12.)

7 (a) *32-bar song form* AABA; each section eight bars long. The B section – usually known as the middle eight – has a contrasting melody, a different chord sequence and sometimes a contrasting key. It sometimes uses different instruments,

and the lyrics may present a different mood or angle from the rest of the song.

(b) **'I got rhythm'** has many points of symmetry, balance, balanced contrast. There should be mention of melodic shapes and chord structure.

8 **'Four'**

Stylistic features of bebop Played by small bands, featuring fast, complex improvisation, sometimes at considerable length. Chords and rhythms generally more complex than in earlier (swing) jazz.

Effects Davis uses Pitch bends, ghost notes, fall-offs (short downward slides), slides or glissandi, double tonguing.

9 (a) *Gospel style* Religious music, often based on hymns but using syncopation, polyrhythms, call and response, improvisation. Clapping, often with up-beat tempos. Often accompanied by piano and/or organ; also drums and or percussion, especially tambourine.

10 **'I'm leavin' you'**

(a) *Stop time* The accompaniment is reduced to a stab on the first beat of each bar, leaving the singer or instrumentalist unaccompanied for a short passage. Heard in Verses 2 and 3.

(b) *Blue notes* Compared with the major scale, certain notes are flattened – usually the 3rd, 5th or 7th. They may be flattened by a semitone or 'bent' by a smaller interval. Heard throughout – the first example is the flattened 3rd (B♭) in Verse 1.

(c) *Lick* A short solo. Heard throughout – the first example is the opening lead guitar lick.

(d) *Triplet* Three notes played in the time of two. Heard throughout – the first example is in Verse 1 on the words 'in the mor-'.

Minor pentatonic scale G B♭ C D F

1950s (page 20)

1 **'Rave on'**

(a) Boogie-woogie rhythm, 12-bar blues (used at start, not throughout), up tempo, strong backbeat, 1950s vocabulary, words such as 'crazy and 'rave'.

(b) *Tempo* Lively, quick, fast, up-tempo.

(c) major

(d) *Syncopation* Off-beat notes are accented.

(e) *Describe ending* Coda: same phrase heard three times. Vocals 'Ah, ah, ah' above a repeated chord sequence (G C G D / I IV I V). Final plagal cadence (C G / IV I) ends sharply on the first beat of the final bar.

2 **'Blue suede shoes'**

(a) *Intro* Unaccompanied vocal entry alternate with striking repeated guitar figure, all strongly marked, in 'stop time'. Establishment of the pulse/beat is repeatedly delayed, building tension. Excitement builds through the words 'One', 'Two', 'Three'.

(b) *Blues influence* Use of 12-bar structure. Blue notes, e.g. opening phrase 'Three to get ready, now go cat go' with flat 7th on the first 'go'. Bluesy guitar licks between vocal phrases, bluesy guitar solos.

(c) Walking bass

(d) During the last twelve bars Perkins repeats the title phrase several times, with a bluesy flattened 3rd on 'shoes'. He ends with a striking, defiant 'You can do anything, but lay off of my blue suede shoes', and this is followed by a falling guitar lick and jazzy final chord with added 6th.

3 **'Maybelline'**

Harsh instrumental sound with clanging guitar flourishes, classic guitar patterns using the bass strings, bluesy rhythm guitar playing, repeated riffs, fast and furious drum-dominated beat, bass line has a country-rock feel. The verses are high-speed narrative, with descriptive detail, the chorus is more expressive and bluesy.

4 **'Move it'**

Up-tempo, high-energy, unsentimental. Clanging guitar opening recalls Chuck Berry. Opening vocal strongly recalls Eddie Cochran's 'C'mon everybody', and general vocal style follows Presley, Cochran, Gene Vincent. Driving bass and guitar. Subject of song is rock 'n' roll.

5 (See model answer for comparison questions on pages 11–12.)

1960s (page 22)

1 **'Stand by me'**

Features typical of soul music Passionate, soulful vocals. Use of strings. I VI II V I chord sequence. Repeated hook line 'Stand by me'.

Form verse and chorus

Beats per bar two or four

Instruments used in intro bass guitar, guiro, bell/Chinese cymbal

Dynamics and instrumentation build up excitement Gradual crescendo. Opening texture sparse, different layers added as song unfolds, e.g. backing vocals and

strings. Tension builds in chorus, which uses a higher range than the verse.
Harmonic scheme Repeated chord sequence

2 **'Can't buy me love'**
Chord sequence of verse 12-bar blues chord sequence (C F7 C G F7 C)
(a) The verse is in the minor and the chorus is in the major
Opening line of chorus Example (c)
Guitar solo Verse 3
One line which uses stop time Towards the end of the verse, on the words 'much for money'

3 **'Help!'**
How is the word 'Help' emphasised? It is usually on the first beat of the bar. Accented chords reinforced by drums are used in the intro, with the pitch rising at each repetition of the word 'Help'. The last 'Help' of the intro is extended into three notes.
Backing vocals Sung in harmony throughout most of the song. Unusual in that the words often anticipate the solo voice rather than echo it.
Form Example (a)

4 **'A day in the life'**
In what ways psychedelic? Examples might include: surreal juxtaposition of subject matter of words and dream theme. Lennon's tape-echoed vocal, rising orchestral glissandi at the end, ambiguity of key and atonal orchestral passages. Drug references such as 'I'd love to turn you on' and 'Had a smoke'. Ambiguous tonality.
Places where music reflects the lyrics Examples might include: alarm clock on the words 'Woke up, got out of bed', the piano concerto chords on the words 'Albert Hall', tremolo semiquavers on the words 'Turn you on'.
Contrasts between verses and middle section Change of key in middle to E major. Middle uses mainly 3rds, verse mainly seconds. Lennon's tape-echoed voice contrasts with the dry sound of McCartney's voice. Inventive drum fills in the verse, steady drum quavers in the middle.
(a) *Orchestra* sparing use: tonal sections and dissonant glissandi
(b) *Piano* Plays throughout most of the song, mostly using regular rhythms. Song ends with an E major chord overdubbed on three pianos.
(c) *Drums* Very sparse at first, building up throughout. Full drum kit enters in verse 2, on the words 'He blew his mind out in a car'. Many inventive fills. Steady quavers in middle section.

5 ***Highway 61 Revisited***
Dylan's first fully electric album, raw driving sound, leaving 'folksinger' image behind. Lyrics vividly poetic/imaginative, expressing emotions including anger, despair – marked rock as a serious art form. This combination of lyrics and rock music, e.g. in title track, inconceivable two years earlier.

6 ***Pet Sounds***
(a) Careful, detailed attention to arrangements and production, making many delicate and pretty effects. Exotic sounds of e.g. bicycle bells, harpsichord, flutes, thérémin, etc. added to the conventional keyboards and guitars, and the multi-layered vocal harmonies associated with the Beach Boys. Each song distinctive in melody and harmonies. Elliptical, sensuous feel to both music and lyrics, moving away from simple, driving pop/rock, e.g. in 'Don't talk'.
(b) *'God only knows'* Many of the qualities mentioned in (a) above. Direct sentiment in lyrics, set to a mellow, lyrical vocal line. Horn solo in introduction. Song brims with invention. Two verses are followed by a wordless vocal bridge. The song ends with a circular chorus with complex vocal counterpoint.

1970s (page 25)

1 **'Teenage kicks'**
New wave is a hybrid of punk and pop – tracks are still short and energetic but more polished and better produced, less aggressive, often more tuneful. Less political than punk, new wave lyrics are more likely to be about adolescent joys and fears.
Intro Two drum beats, then a repeated chord sequence continuing into the verse. Regular rhythm with straight repeated quavers on hi-hat.
Beats per bar Two in a bar or a quick four
Tempo Moderately quick
First phrase shape (a)

2 (See model answer for comparison questions on pages 11–12)

3 **'Winner takes it all'**

Success-elements Songwriting and production skills, vocal sound, catchy tunes, kitsch image

Opening Piano and strings

Rhyme scheme Rhymes come halfway through lines, e.g. 'I figured it made sense, building me a fence'

Drums enter Verse 2

Keyboard sounds Piano, harpsichord

Melody Divided into short phrases. Follows scheme A B A B C C1. Much use of the interval of a 2nd, and of sequences.

Catchy elements The 'Winner takes it all' hook. Repetition in the chord sequence and the melody.

Prominent intervals (b) second

Form Intro Verse Verse Verse Verse Coda (might also be considered as Intro Verse Chorus Verse Chorus Verse Chorus Verse Chorus Coda, if the last lines of the verse are considered to be the chorus.)

Ending Coda – repeat to fade on the words 'So the winner takes it all'

4 **'Tupelo honey'**

How is variety achieved? Vocal improvisation. Also variation in the bass, guitar counter-melody, contrasting instrumental section.

(a) Soulful voice, use of horn section and backing vocals

(b) Use of improvisation

(c) Use of major pentatonic scale

Texture Ever-changing. Sparse at first – voice and accompaniment – then contrapuntal passage with guitar and sax interweaving melodies. Texture becomes gradually richer and more dense, then sparse before building up again.

5 Two albums by **David Bowie**

List A: both concept albums from Bowie's earlier period. Solid rock, relentless beat, hooks and riffs, often rising to melodramatic climaxes. Mick Ronson's guitar a vital element of the sound, plus the sometimes bizarre, sometimes jazz-influenced flourishes of pianist Mick Garson.

List B: In the late 1970s Bowie worked with Brian Eno, experimenting with electronic music. Innovative, including 1977 album *Heroes*, where on 'Moss garden' Bowie plays Japanese koto to Eno's electronic accompaniment. 1975 album *Young Americans* is based on Philadelphia soul. *Diamond Dogs* has a doom-laden sound, with ideas borrowed from George Orwell, of a world of dictatorship and oppression.

6 **'Reynardine'** / other Fairport Convention song

Folk rock Combines folksong, or elements of folk style or instrumentation, e.g. violin, mandolin, with the amplification and drum beats of rock. Examples could include songs from *Liege and Lief* by Fairport Convention.

'Reynardine' features Sandy Denny singing a faithful version of the traditional folk song. In the background the song is punctuated by electric guitar and drum-kit, with psychedelic effects.

7 ***What's Going On***

(a) *What's Going On* is more jazz-influenced, using jazz-inspired rhythms and improvisation. More political, looking at a troubled America torn apart by war, poverty, and prejudice. Less poppy, less dancy. Longer, more extended songs.

(b) On 'Save the children' Gaye's voice is overdubbed throughout the song. It opens in a minor key with Gaye speaking the lyrics backed by a wordless choir and low strings. Next he adds a vocal overdub, duetting with himself, one part spoken and the other singing jazzy responses. The sung vocal line become more intense and soulful as the texture becomes more complex.

1980s (page 28)

1 **Siouxsie and the Banshees**

'Love in a void' is straightforward punk, whereas 'Playground twist' and 'Happy house' have a darker feel with their use of wailing voices and doleful, obsessive lyrics.

2 **'Love can't turn around'**

Elements typical of house Snare drum rolls, programmed hi-hats, pummelling drum machines, orchestral 'stab' samples.

4 **'You think you're a man'** / other HiNRG song

Musical characteristics and origin of HiNRG Came from disco, but faster and more synthesizer-orientated, with high energy, frenetic bass lines and drum machines, influenced by Giorgio Moroder.

5 **'How soon is now'** / other Smiths song
(a) *Features of Smiths style* Lyrics sensitive and thoughtful, mainly concerned with shyness and unrequited love in everyday England. 1960s-influenced sound. Morrissey's mournful, occasionally falsetto croon. Sophisticated, melodic guitar style of Marr. The lyrics of 'How soon is now', combined with Morrissey's gloomy voice, paint a picture of unbearable loneliness. Everyday anti-image, the opposite of macho rock imagery.
(b) Jangly guitars, unglamorous style and thoughtful lyrics are all typical of 1980s indie style.

6 **'Summer of 69'**
(a), (c) and (f)

7 **'Cars'** / other Gary Numan song
Hallmarks of Gary Numan's style Robotic vocal delivery and cold, detached lyrics. Synthesizer band with keyboard synthesizers, drum machine and synthesizer effects. Songs based on simple short repeated patterns, riffs and chord sequences.

8 **Joy Division**
Sombre, stripped-down sound, dark, unsettling lyrics. Ian Curtis's low and unusual voice combined with Peter Hook's prominent melodic bass guitar style results in a deep, murky sound. Curtis's suicide in 1980 added to the sombre image.

9 **'I should be so lucky'** / other 1980s Stock, Aitken and Waterman song
The songs are catchy and easy to sing. Strong hooks (e.g. 'I should be so lucky; lucky, lucky, lucky'). S, A and W had over 140 hits for artists such as Kylie Minogue, Jason Donovan, Sonia, Rick Astley.

1990s (page 31)

1 **'Killing in the name'**
(a) *Derived from metal* Thrash-like riffs, power chords, high volume and electric guitar distortion, drum rolls and simple driving rhythms. Screaming raspy vocals in the first half of the song.
(b) *Derived from rap* Political anti-establishment words. Rhythmic rapping vocals in the second half of the song.

2 **'Stan'**
Main ingredients Dido 'Thank you' song, rap narrative, sound effects, guitar, bass guitar, drums.
Bass line Same pattern repeated throughout
Lyrics Urban US culture, violent hard-hitting lyrics about death and murder – an account of an obsessive fan who kills himself by driving into a river with his pregnant girlfriend trapped in the car boot.
Main interest Narrative of the lyrics, juxtaposition with the haunting verse from 'Thank you'.
Use of sound effects To illustrate the story, e.g. girlfriend screaming, car crash.
DJ-ing techniques Scratching, mixing the two tracks – Dido and Eminem.

3 **'Let me entertain you'**
Style Pure pop
Beats per bar Four
What makes it sound energetic? Rapid tempo, fast beat, plenty of movement, lots happening throughout e.g. different instruments entering.
How is excitement built up through the intro? Opens with a long, sustained note which gradually gets louder, then the texture builds up as instruments enter one by one – tambourine, piano, guitar – eventually all playing together when the voice enters.
Interval used in chorus second
Hook Short, catchy melodic or rhythmic idea, instantly memorable.
Verse and chorus rhythms Verse: mainly short, syncopated notes. Chorus: longer sustained notes.
Use of dynamics Excitement built up through use of crescendos, e.g. in the intro.
How many chords three
Instruments apart from guitar and drums piano, tambourine, trumpets

4 **'Angels'**
Interval between first two notes sixth
Vocal register change On the words '... all she offers me protection'.
Tempo Quite slow, c. 76 bpm or crotchets per minute.
Climax Opens quietly with piano and strings, then the instrumentation builds up in layers. After a crescendo a drum kit is added and gradually becomes more prominent. Vocals move into a higher register. Dynamics build up throughout the song. A guitar solo is heard at the high point.

5 **'Can't get you out of my head'**
Catchy elements The la la la refrain and the words 'Can't get you out of my head', set to a simple 3-note melody.
Words reflected in the accompaniment Long note on the word 'stay'; the words 'ever and ever' are repeated several times.

6 **'Don't look back in anger'**
Britpop A nostalgic movement looking back to the heyday of British pop music in the 60s and bands like the Kinks, the Who and especially the Beatles. It often uses straightforward chord sequences, verse and chorus, backing vocals, and guitars and drums line-up.
Beatles influences Opening piano chords recall Lennon's 'Imagine'. Use of backing vocals. Use of Lennon's words 'start a revolution from my bed'.
Texture Rich/dense, with chiming, jangly guitars.
Climax The instrumental towards the end of the song – guitar solo which gradually gets louder and more complex, ending with a drum flourish.
Changes in the last few bars The song becomes quieter and slower. The texture thins down as instruments drop out.

7 **'Common people'**
Britpop features Verse and chorus structure, traditional chord sequences, nature of lyrics (social observation; words describe everyday life), strong melodic vocal line.

8 ***Discreet Music*** **and** ***Music for Airports***
Conceived as background music rather than for conscious listening, a collage of gently moving phrases and slowly evolving soundscapes.

9 **'Killing me softly with his song'**

Roberta Flack (1973)	Fugees (1996)
Instrumentation Electric piano, drums/perc, etc, but generally discreet.	Heavier drum sound, brief but obvious sitar.
Vocals/Backing vocals Solo line soulful, laid back, intimate. Gospel-influenced backing vocals, with reverb. Verse 4 scat-sung to 'oh' and 'la'.	More vocal layers, some harmonising with the melody, some elaborating it. Overlapped overdubs of lead vocal. Hip-hop/rapped interjections.
Texture Generally light.	Denser, more rhythm-oriented.
Dynamics Generally gentle, quiet feel throughout. Verse 4 slightly louder.	Bigger bass and drum sound gives generally louder impression.
Style Intimate ballad, with soulful lead vocal. Gentle Latin sound to percussion accompaniment.	Transformed into a slow dance track. Vocal style more mannered, with added decoration and vibrato.
Form Verse and chorus.	Follows original, with some cut-and-paste.

The History of Recording (page 34)

1 **'West End blues'**
Limited frequency response, mainly focused in the mid range. Some distortion. Some instruments not clearly in focus. The recording is in mono.

2 **'That's all right'**
(a) Twelve-bar blues chord progression, 'black' style of singing, use of 'blue' notes in both the vocal and the guitar tracks, 'chugging' rhythm section.
(b) Recording lacks the crystal clarity of present day recordings. Recorded live. Mono.

3 **'River deep – mountain high'**
Phil Spector was a successful record producer whose distinctive sound was called the 'wall of sound'. This rich texture used echo, tape loops, multi-layering and a powerful backbeat. Large musical forces employed, including large groups of backing singers, string and brass sections and multiple percussionists. He tended to push each track to its limit, giving a 'saturated' production quality.

4 **'New rose'** and **'Anarchy in the UK'**
'New rose' Tribal drums, simple riffs
'Anarchy in the UK' Very different sound – anthemic, multi-tracked guitars and accomplished production: richer, warmer, more mainstream than 'New rose'.

5 **Pink Floyd / punk**
(a) Pink Floyd used the studio very much as an instrument in its own right – evident in the use of FX, tape editing, crossfades to merge songs, sequenced synthesizers, much overdubbing, general lush and warm quality of the recording. The production, even today, sounds clean and highly polished.
(b) Punk tracks tended to be recorded live in the studio – little used in the way of FX to warm up the sound. Leaving the recording 'bare' helped create feeling of rawness and aggression. It was also a reaction to the excesses of production used by prog rock bands such as Pink Floyd, Yes and Genesis.

6 **George Martin**
Production skills These include:
Techniques: interesting use of stereo field on most tracks, partly owing to the lack of tracks onto which to record (*Sgt. Pepper* was recorded using 4-track technology), i.e. many parts had to be bounced down onto single tracks. This process was carefully managed to reduce build-up of tape hiss, resulting in a surprisingly clear recording.
Effects: delay (harp on 'She's leaving home', vocal on 'Mr. Kite'), sound FX (crowds cheering, cock-crow on 'Pepper', jet noise on 'Back in the USSR' etc.)
Tape editing: 'Mr. Kite', 'Revolution 9'
Vocals (backing vocals especially) recorded at various speeds to thicken texture ('Lucy in the sky')
Use of string and brass arrangements to enhance Beatles' own musical contributions ('Day in the life', 'Good night').

7 **'Two tribes'**
Horn defined mid-80s sound: chunky, funky drums, Fairlight samples, producing enormous soundscapes of pristine sound quality. Quite heavy use of FX throughout, including delay, reverb, chorus. Lush, rich productions allowed Horn to be described as a sort of 80s Phil Spector.

8 **'It's a sin'**
Sequenced sound very indicative of this decade: bubbling synths, splashy electronic snares, four-on-the-floor, disco-derived groove all typical of Pet Shop Boys' output. This use of technology clearly differentiates this recording from those of the 50s. Harmonies also more complex than the 3-chord blues patterns of the 50s.

9 **'Common people'**
Use of synthesizers, compression of recording in general and vocal in particular, wide use of reverb for a slightly 60s feel, distortion on guitar parts, doubletracking of the vocal line, overdubbing of guitar parts.

Acoustic Instruments (page 35)

1 **'Black and tan fantasy'**
Techniques in the brass solos Plunger mute, growling, pitch bends, glissandi or slides.

2 **'Tupelo honey'**
Wind instr Flute, alto saxophone. Flute used in intro, playing a slow, simple 8-note melody, then repeated. This returns at end of song. Sax plays an improvised solo after verse/chorus 2.
Transposing instr Alto saxophone: in E♭, sounding a major 6th below the written pitch.

3 **'Trenchtown rock'**
Bass drum beats 2 and 4 of each bar
Snare drum Used to play fills, e.g. at the very beginning. The rim is used most of the time, except for particular accents.

Electronic Instruments (page 37)

1 **'Star spangled banner'**
Techniques feedback, string bends, slides, whammy bar, divebombing, hammer-ons, pull-offs

2 **Van Halen**
Techniques feedback, string bends, slides, whammy bar, divebombing, hammer-ons, pull-offs, fretboard tapping

3 **'Nutbush city limits'**
Effects used fuzz, wah-wah (the difference between fuzz and overdrive is that fuzz is created by FX pedal transistor distortion, whereas overdrive refers to 'overdriven' valve amps i.e. the guitar's output overloads/overdrives the valve preamp stage or valve power stage of an amplifier.)
Guitar riff

4 ***Switched On Bach***
(a) Carlos does not attempt to mimic the original instrumentation but presents new sounds. Carlos recordings tend to be faster than 'straight' versions, giving them a lively, bubbling quality. Individual lines are easily heard, due to clarity of the electronic sounds. The recordings are faithful to the original scores.
(b) *Possible reasons for preferring originals* More 'live' feel, more 'human'. Matches composer's intentions.
Possible reasons for electronic versions Innovative soundscapes, clarity of line, creative use of stereo field.
Moog Keyboard instrument using voltage-controlled oscillators, filters and envelope generators to synthesize sounds. These can be patched together in various ways, e.g. the envelope shaper can control the filter, or a low frequency oscillator (LFO) can control another oscillator to produce vibrato.

Digital Technology (page 38)

1 **'This corrosion'**
Grandiose, including New York Choral Society. Steinman typically uses multitracked guitar lines, heavy reverb (particularly on drums for a big 'splashy' sound), carefully controlled use of a wide dynamic range.

2 **'Heartbreak Hotel'**
Early echo and reverb effects were produced by feeding a signal from the desk to a speaker placed in an echo chamber, an enclosed space which had the right acoustical properties. Microphones then picked up the echoed sound, which was fed back to the desk. Later devices created the same effect by using tape loops running through both recording and playback heads (as in the WEM Copicat). Digital signal processing is now the standard means of producing these effects.

3 **Human League**
Multi-layered monophonic synths and synthetic percussion sounds, combined with basic sequencing techniques, form the essence of Human League's sound. Because the synths are monophonic, the texture focuses on contrapuntal lines rather than harmony, and the sounds used are quite stark. Reverb is used to soften the hard electronic edge and add an air of mystery to the track.

4 **'Pump up the volume'** or **'Theme from S'Express'**
'Pump up the volume' Cut-and-paste approach, jumping between different breaks. Eclectic selection of samples, including wailing sound and guitar feedback.
'Theme from S'Express' Uses intro synth and brass hook from 'Is it love you're after' (Rose Royce). Adds vocal samples.

Style and Structure (page 41)

1 **'Rock around the clock'**
Intro Crisp drum opening. 'Stop time' approach with vocalist very clear. Simple concept: One, two, three o'clock, four o'clock, rock' etc. set on a rising arpeggio.
Turnaround The final part of a section, in which the melody or chords prepare for the next section by providing a smooth transition.
Riff A short, repeated melodic pattern, often forming the background to a solo or vocal line. Usually 2–4 bars long. Often in the bass. May be heard at different pitches to fit in with the harmony; may also change its shape slightly.
Turnaround at end of song shape (b)

2 **'Maybe baby'**
Describing structure using letters Intro A A B A A′ B A outro (or coda).
Close harmony When the voices are close together in pitch.
Contrast in the middle eight It moves to the subdominant chord.

3 **'I want to hold your hand'**
Vocals harmony vocals added
Drum part hi-hat is closed; much clearer texture
Lyrics sentiment is taken further, made more personal
Harmony modulates (to subdominant); different chords

4 **'Waterloo sunset'**
Bass line opening (b) Descends stepwise
Form of verse (c) AABA
Middle eight Contrasting section in the middle of a song (not necessarily eight bars long), often with different instrumentation and/or key. The words may also have a different subject. Sometimes referred to as the 'bridge'. Found e.g. between verses 2 and 3.
Drum fill A short decorative solo which breaks the drum pattern. Found throughout e.g at 'And they don't need no friends'.
Guitar lick A short guitar solo. Heard at the end of some of the sung phrases e.g. after the words 'flowing into the night' and 'light shines so bright'.
Backing vocals Occur throughout the song. They echo the words of the singer or sing 'oo's and 'sha la la's.

5 **'You've got a friend'**
Features of singer-songwriter style
Introspective, thoughtful lyrics and expression. Gentle sound, often with folky acoustic guitar accompaniment. Little use of percussion. Sometimes jazz-influenced harmonies.
Other American singer-songwriters of the 1970s
Answers might include Joni Mitchell, Carole King, Randy Newman, Loudon Wainwright III, Laura Nyro, Carly Simon.

6 **'Soul man'**
Atlantic/Stax sound Horn section used round core rhythm-unit of guitar, bass and drums. Rhythm-unit very closely knitted. Very crisp rhythmic playing, short phrases, high energy, very danceable.
How many verses three
Middle eight Two minutes into the song, after verse and chorus have each been heard three times.
Change of key Immediately after the middle eight.

7 **Bob Marley**
Answers might include the following: laid-back tempo; bass drum plays on beats 2 and 4; rim shots used on snare; dominating bass guitar sound; guitar plays on the off beat, often uses upstrokes; relaxed but very rhythmic, very danceable.

8 **'Trenchtown rock'**
Tempo c. 150 bpm
Beats per bar four
Improvisation Where musicians make the music up as they are performing. Heard in the middle sections of this song.
Form (b) Verse and chorus major; middle sections use minor chords.
Material for outro from middle section

9 **'Get up (I feel like being a) sex machine'**
Groove-based Long sections where the same rhythm parts repeat for dancing.
Horn stabs A stab is an accented single note or chord.
Piano riff A riff is a short, repeated melodic pattern, often forming the background to a solo or vocal line. Usually 2–4 bars long. May be heard at different pitches to fit in with the harmony; may also change its shape slightly.
(c) The song uses only two chords.

10 **'Disco inferno'**
Elements typical of disco music Four-on-the-floor drumbeat, hedonistic lyrics, lush instrumentation including strings and horns, lively bass line combining with drums to make a strong dance beat.
Instruments Strings, clavinet (an electronic keyboard instrument), horns, guitar (especially with wah-wah).
Intro Begins with a crashing cymbal followed by a flurry of violins and a driving descending line which gathers momentum as it moves into the verse groove.
Groove-based Long sections where the same rhythm parts repeat for dancing
The chorus appears first.
Harmony (b) Verse based on one minor chord, chorus uses major chords.

11 **'Holidays in the sun'**
(a) *Vocal style* sneering vocals, sometimes reinforced by shouted backing vocals
(b) *Instrumentation* two guitars, drums
(c) *Lyrics* The final section in particular uses stream-of-bile vocals.
(d) *Tempo* fast and energetic
(e) *Guitar solo* no frills, very direct, one repeated continuous phrase
(f) *Texture* riff-based, dense texture produced by buzz-saw guitar sound, use of distortion and feedback

12 **'Smells like teen spirit'**
Excitement generated in intro A riff is played by a single guitar, then repeated by the whole band – all the energy is released when the riff kicks in.
Rhythm of opening riff example (a)
Dynamics soft verses, loud choruses
Guitar material follows melody and structure of verse and bridge

13 **'Bring the noise'**
Second rapper Doubles the last word of some lines, adds spoken ad libs and answering phrases.
How typical of 1980s hip-hop? Rhythmical rhyming rapping using two vocalists; rhetoric-filled lyrics; samples, DJ-ing, remixing, scratching, background collage.

14 **'Independent women Pt 1'**
Key features of R&B Soul-styled, semi-improvised vocals; an economical, funky riff; stuttering, staccato programmed drums and bass; call-and-response vocals; disco influenced strings.
Variations in chorus Increasingly virtuosic vocals, both in the elaboration of the lead line and the added harmonies.
Call and response Soloist sings a phrase to which a larger group responds with an answering phrase.
Middle eight Uses *a cappella* vocal harmonies plus gospel-like wordless vocal improvisation.

15 **Big beat**
Heavily sampled-oriented combination of hip-hop breaks and rock 'n' roll sensibilities with modern dance sonorities. Tempo usually around 100–140 bpm.

16 **'Renegade master'**
Interest Generated through varied use of samples, timbre, rhythms, lyrics. Texture varies with drums sometimes dropping out.

17 **'Access'**
Bass drum pattern Plays on all four beats ('four-on-the-floor')
Instrument with main pulse synthesizer
Instrument at start drums/percussion
Pedal note a continuous single note, in this case on high strings
Climax from 4:06
How achieved? It is preceded by the breakdown section, which builds up from just strings and vocal samples, adding synth riff, filtered to rise steadily in pitch and accompanied by a snare drum roll, leading in to the climax at 4:06.
Instrument in mix out drums

Index

Artists are listed under surname (e.g. Hendrix, Jimi) or the first part of their stage name (e.g. Boy George is indexed under Boy). Album titles (and also film titles) are in *italics*. Page numbers in brackets refer to answers. Where two page numbers are linked, for instance 25(55), this indicates a question (on 25) and its answer (on 55).

Pop Music: The Text Book

Julia Winterson, Peter Nickol, Toby Bricheno

Pop music is now a component of many courses in schools, colleges and universities, as well as a fascinating subject for the general reader.

Pop Music: The Text Book traces the development of pop music from the beginning of the twentieth century to the present day, investigating the influence of each generation upon the next.

- identifies the forms and musical characteristics of different styles
- includes extensive chapters on the development of music technology
- examines the different roles of people working in the music industry and explains the processes involved in making and selling a CD

LONDON · FRANKFURT · LEIPZIG · NEW YORK
www.editionpeters.com

EP 7690
ISBN 1-84367-007-0